Communication Strategies in Medical Settings

Consciousness and Human Systems

Edited by Dagmar Eigner, Günther Fleck,
Shulamith Kreitler and László Ropolyi

Volume 3

PL ACADEMIC RESEARCH

Katalin Varga

Communication Strategies in Medical Settings

Challenging Situations and Practical Solutions

Medical reader: Judit Schlanger

PL ACADEMIC RESEARCH

Bibliographic Information published by the Deutsche Nationalbibliothek

The Deutsche Nationalbibliothek lists this publication in the Deutsche Nationalbibliografie; detailed bibliographic data is available in the internet at http://dnb.d-nb.de.

Library of Congress Cataloging-in-Publication Data

Varga, Katalin (Psychology professor), author.
Communication strategies in medical settings : challenging situations and practical solutions / Katalin Varga ; medical reader, Judit Schlanger.
p. ; cm. – (Consciousness and human systems, ISSN 1866-668X ; volume 3)
Includes bibliographical references and index.
ISBN 978-3-631-66245-8 (alk. paper) – ISBN 978-3-653-05313-5 (e-book)
I. Title. II. Series: Consciousness and human systems. v. 3. 1866-668X
[DNLM: 1. Communication--Case Reports. 2. Professional-Patient Relations--Case Reports. 3. Public Relations–Case Reports. W 62]
RA423.2
362.101'4–dc23
2015023996

ISSN 1866-668X
ISBN 978-3-631-66245-8 (Print)
E-ISBN 978-3-653-05313-5 (E-Book)
DOI 10.3726/978-3-653-05313-5

PL Academic Research is an Imprint of Peter Lang GmbH.

Peter Lang – Frankfurt am Main · Bern · Bruxelles · New York · Oxford · Warszawa · Wien

This publication has been peer reviewed.

www.peterlang.com

Table of Contents

Introduction

This book presents cases where establishing initial rapport was delayed, disturbed or was complicated by a special circumstance: the patients were agitated, hostile, demanding or just not in control of their consciousness.

Appropriate communication strategies can be applied successfully to solve such situations / cases.

Each and every case presented in this volume with its review is real and happened in everyday medical practice. Most of them have already been published. The cases were subsequently recorded in writing, so certain details might be altered along with the distortion of memory. However, since all colleagues are trained professionals of suggestive communication, they are more likely to remember the consciously formulated phases than average.

Readers will see that there is no generally applicable recipe for such cases.

The solutions presented in this book helped to reach the desired outcome for the certain professional who noted them down. For someone else, a different approach would perhaps work.

It is worthwhile to note that the adequate solution sometimes unfolds only after several trials and after experimenting with different approaches. It does not mean that it was a failure if we have to change to another method.

The process by its nature is **interactional**: the expert always has to watch out for the cues indicating what the most suitable strategy would be for that particular patient, in that particular case, and under the given circumstances.

Although in most cases the following steps can be observed:

- the recognition of negative trance state
- building rapport
- (conscious) application of suggestions

Let us see these steps in more detail:

Trance and its Types

"Trance" in the present context may indicate any altered state of consciousness. That is, any situation when the patient's state of consciousness is not rational, reality-oriented or structured. Trance is characterised by a focused state of consciousness and a temporary detachment from reality. An important feature of trance is that one's sensitivity to suggestions is increased and this makes suggestive communication an effective tool in solving difficult situations in negative trance.

It makes a lot of difference what causes and what rules the trance. We talk about **negative** trance when the patients' attention is concentrated on pain, fear, and anxiety, and they do not know where they are or what is happening to them.

In a **positive trance** patients are also focused: this time, however, their body and mind is peaceful and their attention is on something pleasant (usually a good memory or a future goal).

In many cases, the crucial thing is to turn a negative trance state into a positive one (or at least to a neutral one). To be able do this, it is inevitable to build and maintain rapport, a specific relationship between the patient and the health care professional.

Rapport and Building Rapport

In this context, "rapport" means that two (or more) people pay attention to each other, cooperate more and more, and synchronise their interactions for a common goal.

In emergency situations, these are usually missing: patients are fully occupied by their own suffering, anxiety, or pain. Health care professionals/experts who look after these patients perform their tasks automatically and the patient's shouts and whines are disturbing them the most, while some experienced ones do not even care about these signals.

Whereas they have (would have) important messages for each other.

The first step is introduction: note that in almost all of the reviewed cases, the experts introduce themselves, no matter how critical the situation is. Neglecting basic elements of initial rapport building rituals would carry unfavourable messages, such as

- the situation is too serious, there is no time for that
- I am not interested in your personality; therefore, I will not show mine.

Rapport building with patients in negative trance usually continues with diverting their attention. In negative trance, patients almost always pay attention to some unfavourable condition: to their pain, anxiety, the panic of people standing around, etc.

We need to catch their attention somehow and direct it to what we are saying and doing. From the point of developing initial rapport, we use suggestions that are adequate for our therapeutic goals (analgesia, blood clotting, relaxation, etc.)

The rapport that has been built should be maintained as well: it should continuously be fostered, conveying to the patient that we are still working for the same goal, that we appreciate cooperation, etc. When our professional role ends, we need to transfer rapport to the person who continues taking care of the patient (another health care professional or relatives).

Suggestions and Their Efficacy

Suggestions are verbal messages that the receiver nonintentionally accepts and follows. Beyond the words, the environment, objects, and nonverbal messages (eye contact, sighs, touches) can have suggestive effect. The person in trance can be highly susceptible to suggestions and sometimes may follow them literally (so called literalism). We have a suggestive effect even if we know nothing about the suggestive method. This is good news from the perspective of positive suggestions, but makes patients defenseless against unfavourable ones.

Through analysing cases, our purpose is to highlight what methods were successful in solving situations. There are several suggestive techniques and strategies. In this book, we introduce those that are used in the reviewed cases. Trained professionals of suggestive communication use these techniques automatically after a while, in a way that no conscious effort is needed. Just like when acquiring a foreign language at a certain level, the initial difficulties with certain structures disappear as they all come naturally.

Initial Situation – Goal

We close the description of cases by listing the elements of the initial, actual state and of the goal.

At the beginning of a critical or difficult situation, most experts using suggestive communication techniques simply become aware of what the initial difficult situation is and also what goal they would like to achieve. Suggestive sentences – after adequate training and practice – come automatically and naturally during usual everyday medical practice.

You will find in black letters on a grey highlight those variations that we frequently hear, but do not recommend. The favourable variations appear in *italics*.

Techniques Presented in the Review of Cases

Although suggestive communication is far from being a mere list of techniques, it is rather an attitude and a stance. In the following, we briefly highlight the suggestive techniques mentioned in the case reviews.

DIRECT SUGGESTION	
The essence of this technique is the clear and unambiguous formulation of the message we want to convey as opposed to an indirect suggestion, where only the several implications carry the message.	
For example:	Instead of:
Your eyes close.	I don't know whether you have ever thought of why it's more comfortable for most patients to undergo treatment with their eyes closed.

DISSOCIATION, DISSOCIATIVE STRATEGY	
The essence of this technique is that the patient is invited to take up the role of an outsider: instead of being a recipient of the things, the patient should observe them from the outside. We can link this to different tasks we give them during the treatment.	
For example:	Instead of:
As a filmmaker, I wonder what camera position you would choose to make a documentary about this therapy / operation / medical treatment.	(we don't say anything)

DOUBLE-BIND	
The essence of this method is to give choices to the patients concerning the smaller details of a question that they otherwise have no choice to make a decision about. (Note: of course this is a *therapeutic* version of the double bind and not the pathological one described by G. Bateson).	
For example:	Instead of:
For which finger do you want the pulsoximeter?	(we don't say anything, just put it on one)

FUTURE ORIENTATION	
The essence of this technique is that we draw the patient's attention to future events and future happenings. This is especially important if the patient believes the given situation to be fatal or has a fear of death (unspoken perhaps), or if the coming period is a difficult one. In such cases, it is good to look ahead and see 'where we are going'. This usually flashes up a positive goal and at the same time, motivates the patient (to stand the interventions, to overcome fears or to get better). (See: goal centering, motivating).	
For example:	Instead of:
How good it will be to be at home for Christmas!	There is a chance that you will survive the operation.

GIVING A SENSE OF CONTROL	
The essence of this technique is that by giving a sense of control to the patients, we take them out of the role of being passive recipients of medical situations. Giving information can serve this purpose too. It is especially effective if the patients can have choices, if we ask for their agreement in certain questions or if we say thank you if they do the things we asked for. Experiencing the lack of control in a negative state is extremely unfavourable and can even be fatal in the long run (learned helplessless).	
For example:	Instead of:
Can I call you by your first name?	Mom, you will get a clyster now.

GOAL CENTERING	
The essence of this technique is to formulate and to put into words the goal of the procedure (intervention, operation, talk, etc.) and also why it is good for the patient. The patient's attention is directed from being stuck in the 'here and now' or from the anguish about the past to a future, more positive goal. (See also: future orientation, positivity, motivating). An important element of building rapport is to outline a mutually accepted goal with the target being to achieve that mutual goal together.	
For example:	Instead of:
I hear from your wife that you have a little garden. You will be there for the spring works.	This fracture is quite serious. It might even take months until you can get on your own feet again.

IMPLICATION	
The essence of this technique is that we imply something in a hidden, unspoken way.	
For example:	Instead of:
One of the most effective methods to relieve you of your complaint is … (implies: there are many effective methods to choose from)	We might try that …

INFORMING	
The essence of this technique is that we give information to the patient regarding what had happened and about the probable events ahead. Of course, the how is the essence. The basic situation is that we talk about the probable outcome in positive terms and do not describe the possible unfavourable results (however, if any circumstance makes it necessary, we have to give information about them as well). Not all patients require factual information and there are even less who can understand the rational and professional language. A well-chosen metaphor (see there) is more effective in most cases.	
For example:	Instead of:
(in case of mechanical ventilation): While your breathing is assisted by the machine, you cannot speak the usual way. As soon as we take the tube out, you will be able to speak again. Until then, there are many ways we can communicate…	We do not give information about why the patient cannot speak as usual: we do not talk about when it will get back to normal.

METAPHORS, ANECDOTES	
The essence of this technique is that we use seemingly irrelevant metaphors or anecdotes. Metaphors can very powerfully convey our messages and most patients take them better than the factual-professional explanations.	
For example:	Instead of:
This is similar to threading beads or to embroidery: the design can hardly be suspected… then it nicely develops and we can be proud of our work.	There are long and tiring treatments ahead of us. I hope you'll have enough patience to go through it all.

MODELLING	
The essence of this technique is that we give a positive example (a model, a pattern): usuallly only verbally and if possible, in flesh-and-blood reality as well. It is very efficient to involve a patient who has already recovered from the same illness as a model. The patients themselves can also be models at times. For example, by recalling the (healthy) times before the illness or by recalling successfully managed situations from the past.	
For example:	Instead of:
The patient with the same problem was just lying on the opposite bed. She is back home now…	(we don't say anything)

MOTIVATING	
The essence of this technique is that we flash to why it is worth it for the patient to cooperate with us and to accept what we have to do anyway accoring to the rules of our profession. Even taking a simple blood preassure, not to mention a long invasive intervention, is much easier if its meaning and goal is clear for the patient (See also: Goal, Future orientation)	
For example:	Instead of:
(at a blood test) We have a look how effectively your boby is using the prescribed medicines.	I'm going to prick your arm, it'll hurt. Or, I'm going to take blood, it'll hurt.

PACING – LEADING	
The essence of this technique is that before giving the key-suggestion (which for the time being would seem too distant or unlikely), at first we follow the patient: we sit where he/she is, we adjust the rhythm of our breathing to his/hers, we use his/her words, etc. During this time, we watch out for the cues that show the patient perceives this acceptance and this getting in tune: because then, we can start the leading phase: we set off to the operating room, we slow the rhythm of our breathing and we present a key-suggestion.	
For example:	Instead of:
(pacing:) I see you are very frightened, no wonder, all this happened so unexpectedly… you need some time to settle your thoughts and feelings. (leading:) Let's see how the treatment can help your earliest recovery.	No need to worry, (hopefully) you will recover.

PARADOX SUGGESTION	
The essence of this technique is that we convey contents that are (seemingly) in contrast with our goals.	
For example:	Instead of :
We forbid the activity / behaviour that we want to achieve: "It is important not to fall asleep immediately after you go to bed."	Subscribing or urging that.

POSITIVITY	
The essence of this method is to express everything that is possible in positive terms.	
For example:	Instead of:
We emphasise what we expect or want: Relax.	Negating what we want to avoid: Don't tighten yourself.

REFRAMING	
The essence of this technique is that we provide a different framework of interpretation to something. A positive interpretation instead of a negative (tragic, disastrous, sinister) one. On the surface, this simply means using a different word. At the same time, the new – favourable – frame of interpretation brings along connected memories, expectations, feelings, etc. Therefore, a successful reframing changes the whole mood of the situation and raises positive expectations.	
For example: Many people notice how exciting it is to experience that the tissues reunite: the feeling of strain, tingle and the like. Isn't it wonderful how our body can heel its tissues?	Instead of : You will experience a sharp pain in the wound for days after the surgery.

REPETITION	
The essence of this technique is to repeat important suggestions as often as possible. Either repeating them word-by-word or using different terms.	
For examle:	Instead of:
Relax… that's very good… just relax… calmly…	Relax! I told you not to tighten!

RHYTHM, PAUSES
The essence of this technique is that we can have more pauses than in everyday spoken language: we pay attention to the rhythm of our utterance. We have to give time to the patients to process what they heard.

RHYTHM, PAUSES (cont.)	
For example:	Instead of:
Bleeding is weakening... weakening... and...slowly... stops...yes...	Bleeding stops.

REALITY ORIENTATION	
It is natural in a trance that the perception of space and time becomes uncertain: the patients do not know where they are or what is happening to them. Listing the mere facts, and even repeateing them, helps restore the real frame of consciousness.	
For example:	Instead of:
You have been transferred to hospital after an accident. You are safe.	(we don't tell this to the patient)

THE PRINCIPLE OF SUCCESIVE APPROXIMATION	
The essence of this technique is that we outline how to achieve the final goal step by step. At the beginning, we formulate only a few things and gradually formulate more and more.	
For example:	Instead of:
As if you were already more tired... yes, you could do with a good sleep. You are yawning already... and will fall asleep soon.	Try to sleep at last!

UTILISATION	
The essence of this technique is that we should utilise every circumstance, even the seemingly disturbing or unfavourable incidents, as something that helps to reach our goal.	
For example:	Instead of:
Every single slam of a door only helps you to relax because it reminds you of how busy other people are and you can relax.	Unfortunately people lack any good manners: they can't use door handles (furiously).

YES-SET	
The essence of this technique is that we bring up ideas that cannot be denied or that there is a good chance for the patient's agreement, and only after this do we give the (essential) target suggestion that we intend to achieve, instead of starting immediately with the target suggestion without any preparation. The 'facts' and 'obvious things' can be as simple as our name or which floor we are going, or that we are just getting into the ambulance car, etc. It is not important to get an obvious, verbal 'yes' from the patient. It is enough if we get an internal nod, a type of agreement, because this is probably how the patient will react to our key message as well.	
For example:	Instead of:
– Do you hear what I'm saying? – I'm XY, an ambulance physician. – I am here to take care of you. – We are transferring you to hospital. – They are already expecting you. (target suggestion): you are safe, just listen to me and do what I'm telling you.	We take care of the patient without any words or without any introduction we only say: – Oh, that is really serious.

Those who have a deeper interest in this method can get further guidance from the literature that has already been published in this topic or from the accredited trainings.

KEKECS Z., VARGA K. (2013) Positive suggestion techniques in somatic medicine: A review of the empirical studies *Interventional Medicine and Applied Science* 5:(3) pp. 101–111.

KEKECS Z., JAKUBOVITS E., VARGA K., GOMBOS K. Effects of patient education and therapeutic suggestions on cataract surgery patients: A randomized controlled clinical trial *Patient Educationand Counseling* (ISSN: 0738-3991) 94: (1) pp. 116–122.

SCHLANGER J., FRITÚZ G., VARGA K. (2013) Therapeutic suggestion helps to cut back on drug intake for mechanically ventilated patients in intensive care unit *Interventional Medicine and Applied Science* 5:(4) pp. 145–152.

SZILÁGYI AK., DIÓSZEGHY C., FRITÚZ G., GÁL J., VARGA K. (2014) Shortening the length of stay and mechanical ventilation time by using positive suggestions via MP3 players for ventilated patients.

Interventional Medicine and Applied Science (ISSN: 2061-1617) (eISSN: 2061-5094) 6: (1) pp. 3–15.

VARGA K. (2012) Suggestive communication with critically ill patients in the context of death and dying. Health Psychology research focus confronting dying and death Ed.: Shulamith Kreitler Nova Science Publishers New York. 293–314.

VARGA K. (2013) Suggestive techniques connected to medical interventions *Interventional Medicine and Applied Science* 5:(3) pp. 95–100.

VARGA K. (ed.) (2011) Beyond the words. Communication and suggestion in medical practice. Nova Science Publisher, New York.

VARGA K., Varga Zs., Fritúz G. (2013) Psychological support based on positive suggestions in the treatment of a critically ill ICU patient: A case report *Interventional Medicine and Applied Science* 5:(4) pp. 153–161.

VARGA K. (2012) Suggestion and Placebo in the Service of Healing: Common Features and Characteristic Differences Shulamith Kreitler, Günther Fleck, László Rapolyi, Dagmar Eigner (eds) Systems of Logic and the Construction of Order, Peter Lang GmbH Internationaler Verlag der Wissenschaften, Frankfurt am Main, 151–169

VARGA K., DIÓSZEGHY CS., FRITÚZ G. (2007) Suggestive Communication with the Ventilated Patient, *European Journal of Mental Health, 2*, 137–147.

The Fist

Original story	Note
A young male patient was taken to the hospital with a dislocated shoulder. He was pale, his blood pressure was high, and his pulse was rapid. He had a lot of pain and he was in a very negative state. This state made it simply impossible to establish a reliable connection. His answer to questions about possible allergies, previous illnesses, and prescribed medication was always 'I don't know'.	
Then I ordered him in an authoritarian style to clench his fist on his healthy side. I repeated it in a powerful tone which allowed no reply: "*Clench it … strongly… clench it…*"	The expected answer was very close to the actual state of the man (**pacing**) so he could accomplish the instruction. The doctor now gained and controlled the patient's attention in the developing cooperation. The command for the strong fist clenching was kept up till the limit of the patient's tolerance.
According to the instructions, he had to clench his fist stronger and stronger for 30 to 60 seconds. Then finally I said in a nice, gentle tone, "*And now you can release it… you can relax every muscle… your whole body… easily… you can close your eyes, if you want and you can feel your body melting into complete relaxation…*"	The sudden shift could be another surprise; binding the patient's attention (again), it was easy to accomplish the suggestions of relaxation (**leading**).

Initial situation	Goal
– Negative trance – Merit connection cannot be established	– Breaking the negative trance and turning it into a positive one – Establishing cooperation

DESCRIBER OF THE CASE: Katalin Bloch-Szentágothai Dr., Anesthesiologist, Hypnotherapist.

THE FIRST EDITION: Bloch-Szentágothai K. (1995) Hypnose in der Anasthesie. Arzt-Gazette Médicale, 16. pp. 7.

Knock-knock, Someone's Tapping on Your Door

Original story	Note
A man in his sixties is admitted to the intensive care unit following complications from his hip operation. He is still half-asleep, but as five to six people rush to treat him and to set the appropriate machines and drains, he firmly resists. A nurse asks me to hold his hand while she takes his blood.	
I start to squeeze his wrist. I try to do it firmly and then I suddenly let it go, which results in him also relaxing his hand.	The synchrony of squeezing-relaxing (**nonverbal pacing-leading**) is only a slight sign of making contact now.
I start to stroke his hand. He relaxes, but gradually he starts to fight back again. This of course is not surprising; a vulnerable, half-unconscious man is being assaulted by multiple painful pokes, strange pulling, and touching from every direction.	
In this chaos, I try to speak to him but it surely is difficult for him to listen. I cannot get near his head either.	There is no physical possibility for verbal communication.
I squeeze his hand again and he relaxes again when I do. During such a break, I start to tap a simple rhythm on his palm. I interrupt the sequence sometimes. In response, he scratches my palm and I stroke his hand.	Remaining in the rhythm of squeezing-relaxing, the specialist starts to tap a simple rhythm on the patient's palm.
When we lose the synchrony as he again becomes tense, I start all over: I squeeze his hand firmly and let it go, he then relaxes and I tap the rhythm on his hand. The same simple rhythm every time. He scratches back.	The tapped 'rhythm' is an unmistakable sign, or simply an intuitive step of the psychologist (it cannot be used as a substitute for verbalism)...
My mind wanders off. He keeps fighting and all I can do is tiredly hang onto his hand.	There is (can be) 'neutral gear' in the communication with the patient.

Original story	Note
Suddenly he relaxes again and I realise he does not just scratch, but he taps the rhythm on my palm.	The patient initiates contact. In this situation, it means a lot: he's managed to filter the flow of stimuli that somebody had been trying to make to establish a connection with him. What's more, he's figured out how to use this information to seek contact himself. This is an excellent **rapport** opportunity for future cooperation.
Connection can be made even under these difficult circumstances.	

Initial situation	Goal
– Patient is not fully conscious following sedation (negative trance) – He does not accept the procedure, but resists	– Make a connection – Relaxation and to build cooperation

DESCRIBER OF THE CASE: Adrienn K. Szilágyi, Clinical Psychologist.

THE FIRST EDITION: Varga K. (ed.) (2011) Beyond the words. Communication and suggestion in medical practice. Nova Science Publisher, New York.

Thrombosis

Original story	Note
During the evening at the emergency ward, the patient came in with a swollen left foot. I examined him and told him that we would have to admit him to the hospital because he had deep vein thrombosis. He didn't want to stay. I informed him that it was in his best interest and for his own safety he would have to stay in the hospital.	The patient doesn't understand what is evident for the doctor; he does not want to stay at the hospital.
"But why?" *"Because you have thrombosis and if we do not start your treatment, the blood clot may dislodge and travel. It may get stuck in your lungs and it may cause severe blockage (so-called pulmonary embolism). You may have heard of this condition. This is a dangerous complication that can be avoided if we treat the clot just discovered in your leg."* "How do you know that I have a clot?" *"From the fact that your leg is swollen and it's painful."* "Isn't there another way to prove this?" *"Yes, there is. "I tell him, "the clot can be confirmed with an ultrasound."* "And if the ultrasound is negative can I go home?" *"No, because in spite of a negative or inconclusive ultrasound, you still might have a thrombosis. We would have to do a lab test. The negative results of that can positively rule out thrombosis."*	The doctor gives logical and professional answers to the continuous questions of the patient (**informing**).
Then the patient asks, "If you do not see it on the ultrasound then why should I believe that I have thrombosis? Is it just a figment of your imagination?"	The patient is hostile, moreover, outright accusatory. Look, I have no time to answer your endless questions!

Original story	**Note**
For which my answer was: *"If on a clear morning, you look out the window but a cloud covers the sun, from the mere fact that there is sufficient light from the direction of the eastern sky you come to the conclusion, that the sun has risen. If the sun emerges from behind the cloud for a moment, then you really have direct proof. Then when it shines on us, we are happier. But on a clear morning without seeing the sun behind the clouds, everybody can righteously believe that the sun shines behind the clouds, right?"*	The key to the solution is a **metaphor.** The detailed elaboration of a motif that significantly differs from the professional answers used earlier, one that seemingly doesn't even belong here. The elements of the metaphor are a point-to-point replication of the situation regarding the patient's diagnosis (imaging among the fields of experience, so-called cross-domain mapping), at the same time excluding the possibility of doubt. With the wording in first person plural, the doctor includes himself and expresses a fellowship with the patient. Even positive feelings can sneak into the situation; the sun shines on us, we are happy (**positivity**).
After this, the patient signed the consent for admission without saying a word and we could start treatment.	What could not be understood with rationality, successfully got through via the language of metaphors adjusted to the actual processing mode of the patient.

Initial situation	**Goal**
– Untrusting and hostile patient – Rational explanations do not work	– Winning his trust – Getting the situation to be understood and accepted

DESCRIBER OF THE CASE: Csaba Diószeghy Dr., Anaesthesiologist-Intensive Therapy and Oxycologist-Emergency Specialist.

THE FIRST EDITION: Case report to this volume.

Truck

Original story	Note
A man, who got trapped under a truck in a traffic accident and suffered multiple injuries, was lying on the road at my surgery.	
I applied a very simple method. *"Do you hear my voice?"* I asked. When he responded, I said, *"I'm a local doctor, and I'm asking you to pay attention to my voice. Listen to what I'm saying...* *Concentrate... concentrate more...even more and more..."*	The establishment of the **rapport** begins with a basic question, which on the one hand clarifies a really important detail (whether the voice of the professional reaches the injured) and on the other hand, it can also function as a **yes-set** element, whose following element is communicating the fact that the speaker is a doctor. In the given situation, the fact that the injured is immediately dealt with by a professional is a circumstance that deepens trust. The patient's attention from the presumed pain is now directed at the doctor herself. The key to the solution in itself is in establishing a **rapport** that someone amid the huge panic is also aware of the person of the injured and professionally applies the alternatives that can function even in such a difficult situation.
"...with every intake of breath, just let the background noises help you to concentrate more and more on what I'm saying."	The noise is terrible here. I hope you can hear me. Additional reinforcement on focusing the attention is needed and at the same time, deepening the positive version of the trance-state. The suggestion also utilises the background noises connected to the accident and the rescue (**utilisation**): far from distracting the patient's attention, they help him concentrate even more.
Then I gave him analgesic and blood- clotting suggestions in order to decrease the blood loss and help stabilise his physical state.	The situation that has been prepared with building the rapport and establishing the yes-set comes to the crucial suggestions, to blood clotting, and analgesia.

Original story	Note
When the ambulance finally arrived, they were surprised at how calm the man was and how stable his fundamental physiological functions (breathing, blood pressure) were. He could be taken to hospital safely.	

Initial situation	Goal
– Negative trance, pain, and blood loss – Presumably, the focus is on the uncomfortable physical symptoms.	– Getting in touch and transforming the negative trance – Blood-clotting and analgesia – Stabilising the state of the patient

DESCRIBER OF THE CASE: Mhairi McKenna Dr., Hypnotherapist.

THE FIRST EDITION: Varga K. (ed.) (2011) Beyond the words. Communication and suggestion in medical practice. Nova Science Publisher, New York.

Nothing Yet

Original story	Note
I met the two crying women at the surgical unit. They were mother and daughter. The 72-year-old father was being resuscitated in the operating room. Around them, there were visitors of other patients. Nobody was communicating with them. The situation was quite tense. Nurses ran in and out of the room and doctors came and went. The mother was diabetic. Her daughter kept asking her if she felt alright. They took turns crying. They also tried to comfort each other in turns.	
I asked if I could sit by them and I introduced myself. "*It must be very hard for you to sit here like this*" I said. Crying and nodding came as the answer.	Luckily, there is someone here who 'notices' the family of the patient as well. Asking for permission to sit (1), introducing herself (**basic rapport building**) (2), as well as the empathetic remark of 'it must be hard to sit here' (**pacing**) (3), together serve as a **yes-set**. Thus, even in this emotionally difficult situation, the cooperation is established between the specialist and the family.
During the conversation with the mother (I thought she was more in need), I got to know the whole story. She told me what happened and when. Being able to vent worked for her. I learned how serious she thought the situation was, and perhaps this way she would not have unrealistic expectations either.	Therefore, the mother's account serves multiple purposes. First, it informs the specialist about the situation. It also gives an opportunity for her to vent and remember how her husband got here, which may turn her expectations regarding the outcome in a more realistic direction.

Original story	Note
A nurse from the operating room shouted out a question about status; the only response from her colleague was 'nothing yet'. The daughter catches this and starts to cry even more loudly.	The situation is – unfortunately – a common example of specialists communicating between each other and ignoring that: (1) the family may hear what they say, and (2) the family may also be interested in the news.
"*We can see they're doing everything they can to help your father*" (I did not want to say more reassuring statements since the positive outcome was not guaranteed at all). They nodded.	These are the congruent and positive bits of comments in this situation. Like the specialist herself cites, it is worth it to note for the future that everything the specialist says can be read in two ways: whether or not the resuscitation is successful. At the same time, the specialist builds herself in as well: 'we can see' means that she is part of the family and that they are not alone. Don't worry!
In the meantime, I got them some water.	A basic gesture that can mean a lot in this situation (and not just in a biological sense).
Then the doctors and nurses turned up. The doctor brought the bad news that they were unable to save the man.	
The family cried. With the help of a nurse, I ushered them into the operating room to give them a chance to say goodbye.	Based on the previous events, the specialist's company can mean a lot in the moments of saying goodbye.
After we came back out, we sat down again. I stayed for a little while, as the daughter asked me to. "*I didn't know your husband before, but I could see on his face just how peaceful he is now.*" "*Yes, he is now in peace and he got rid of his pain. He was a very good man.*"	It is especially important for the specialist to stay with the family even when it does not seem necessary since they have already said goodbye to the man. The specialist is honest again and says something positive in this situation based on her own experience. This again brings out the agreement from the wife. The fact that she talks about her husband in the past tense is the first sign of acceptance of the situation.

Original story	Note
When her daughter returned, she told her mother that this situation had to be accepted. Everybody passes on eventually.	The mother acknowledges her daughter's statements.
When they sat face-to-face and the daughter assured her mother that they were there for each other, I decided to say goodbye and leave.	The mother's and daughter's attention turn towards each other. This is where the specialist's role ends (with them). Now it is worth it for the specialist to search for an opportunity to elaborate the situation for herself as well.

Initial situation	Goal
– Despair of the family and then negative trance in the bereavement that begins	– Provide support – During the situation: communicate regardless of the outcome – After the death: support them in accepting it and start the bereavement process

DESCRIBER OF THE CASE: Zsuzsa Pazonyiné Balázs; Mental Hygienist.

THE FIRST EDITION: Exam paper for the postgraduate training program on Suggestive Communication in Somatic Medicine, co-organised by the Hungarian Association of Hypnosis and Semmelweis University School of Medicine, Budapest.

Thirsty Earth

Original story	Note
Zsófi is 19 years old. She arrived at my office with her mother after hours on a Friday. They were sitting quietly in the waiting room and breathlessly waited for somebody to come out of the office. However, nobody was inside the office any longer. We had already gone home. When I faced the patient who was waiting for me, thousands of thoughts ran through my head (*"Why now, when the office hours are over? I am in a hurry; I have an appointment; Why didn't she come in in the morning?")*. Zsófi was sitting there with a ghastly pale face. Her frail body – thin as a rail – could hardly hold itself upright and she was close to fainting.	The patient arriving after consultation hours on a Friday understandably does not initially evoke positive affections from the doctor. It is important to conceptualise the negative emotions in connection with this – for herself only, of course. This way, there is a smaller chance (or no chance at all) to let the tension sink in, and this facilitates better concentration on her tasks or the patient.
Her mother said that Zsófi had gone to see a periodontist approximately five years ago for the first time. She had a bad experience and thus she since doesn't know what is going on with her teeth. *"She is terrified,"* added the mother. She didn't have significant pain, but her teeth were occasionally sensitive. They had been planning to come in for a long time, but it was not easy to build Zsófi up for the ordeal. Until this time, Zsófi did not say a word. I was asking myself if perhaps it might be better to talk to Zsófi alone, without her mother's presence. The problem solved itself when Zsófi's mother suddenly announced she was as afraid as Zsófi and therefore she would rather stay in the waiting room.	The mother is the 'spokesperson,' which makes it obvious that she has the rapport with the girl.
I had to escort Zsófi into the office. She seemed to be in need of actual physical support. My ruffled thoughts were smoothed as I observed her terrified state of mind and her physical pain caused by her fear of the dental office. My tension was replaced by the intent to help.	It is needles to fear so much! 'Fortunately' the signs of the patient's negative trance turn the expert's attitude around.

Original story	Note
She sat in the chair and we began to get to know each other. After finding out that there was no need for acute care, we agreed that during this first session, we would just talk to get to know each other, the environment, and our plans.	Knowing the background: it can be especially strange that the precious early Friday night is 'only' spent talking. But it is well compensated by the easy cooperation later on. The phrase 'our plans' in first person plural and now refers to the things to be done together (cooperation). The word 'plan' is preferable to 'treatment' for example, and especially to phrases like 'pulling' or 'filling' (**reframing**).
It turned out that Zsófi had not socialised since the age of 15. Sometimes it was hard for her to even get out of bed. She used to have psychotherapy but she stopped a while ago for different reasons. At home, she helps with her mother's work on the computer. She hadn't wanted to come here but with great efforts she admitted that sooner or later she would have needed it, one way or another. (I made a mental note, "possibly coming here at the end of the office hours she made sure that nothing would be done to her"). She also said that she had already been to a dentist before. She then charmingly added with a smile that no treatment had been done because she had not actually entered the dentist's office. So Zsófi let me know that she was aware of the importance of dental care but she was unable to open her mouth and obviously, coming here was extremely difficult and nearly impossible for her. We talked for about an hour. Then I realised that she had chosen the best time of the day because we would not have had time for this in the middle of the office hours.	The developments propose the question of competence-limits: how far should a dentist go in the treatment of psychological problems (too)? The expressed impulses appear again (properly).

Original story	Note
I built a lot of self-strengthening and motivating suggestions into this conversation, which I repeated when she was leaving. The essence was based on facts: *"You have already made the first and most difficult step: you managed to get here. Take a good look around: can you see anything that catches your eyes as a pleasing surprise? Think it over and you will be able to find more and more pleasing details in being here. You will make me very happy if you recall more of them the next time we meet: let me know what is important to you. And moreover, when you go home, think about it. Or maybe you can practice how wide you can open your mouth for the next time, within your comfort level. It's up to you. You make the decisions."*	The whole suggestion-sequence is foreshadowing, phrased according to cooperation (**future orientation, building of rapport**). The expert utilises every possibility to call attention to the favourable, pleasant experiences (**positivity**): 'you are able to', 'next time', 'pleasing', etc. She bounds it to the undeniable fact: the most difficult step was that she actually made it to the dentist's office.
That was the starting point. Nowadays, Zsófi comes alone to her appointments. She is still anxious, but she opens her mouth readily and unconditionally. She does what she is asked to do. We have since completed a root canal procedure and we have done several fillings. Zsófi's soul inhales the positive suggestions with round, wide-open eyes, like dry earth drinking fresh spring-water. She obviously needs it. She smiles and it cultivates her feeling of safety. This mustn't be forgotten, even for a minute in her case. In the present situation, Zsófi needs support. Her mother promised that they would go back to the interrupted psychotherapy. Her dentist phobia again called the attention to her basic illness.	Although the dentist is aware of the limits of his/her own competence, it is obvious that the information conveyed in connection with the dental treatment has positive effects on the patient's psychological development. At the same time, it is important to include the professional psychotherapeutical treatment.

Initial situation	Goal
– Anxious and even phobic patient – Strong emotional bond with the escorting mother	– Building of rapport (and cooperation) – Releasing fear

DESCRIBER OF THE CASE: Éva Radányi Dr., Dentist and Periodontist.

THE FIRST EDITION: Varga K. (ed.) (2011) Beyond the words. Communication and suggestion in medical practice. Nova Science Publisher, New York.

Let's Drop the Formal Stuff

Original story	Note
I was called in to see an 18-year-old patient who had lost consciousness supposedly as a result of heroin overdose. When he was found in a gateway in Budapest, he had been flat on his side for so long that his left arm had gangrened and had to be amputated from the shoulder down. The young man spent two weeks in coma. After the surgery was carried out, I was called in because he was extremely depressed and had suicidal urges. All this was probably a consequence of the loss of his arm, since his drug withdrawal symptoms coincided with the coma period and thus, he probably did not experience them. When I entered his room in the intensive care unit, he was sitting in a wheelchair with his head bent down. As I walked up and sat down next to him, he barely looked up at me.	
I introduced myself, then asked: *"How do you think we could cooperate more efficiently: if we are on a first-name basis or otherwise, on a formal platform?"* (He chose the first-name basis option).	Initiating contact starts with the introduction (establishing **rapport**), which is followed by a question (**double-bind**). It is indifferent which of the offered alternatives the patient may choose, as what matters is the unquestionable success of the cooperation. Furthermore, the starter question immediately suggests a longer cooperation (implication), which, in the current situation, projects an essential perspective toward the future for the patient.

Original story	Note
"What do your friends call you?" (He told me). *"Can I call you that, too?"* (He nodded).	The questions continue. The professional asks for permission to call the patient by the same name his friends call him. A negative answer is very unlikely for this question, and with the positive reply, he "said yes" to the covert message (**implication**) that the cooperation would be amicable.
With these introductory questions, which on the surface only laid down the frame of our cooperation, an honest, or even pleasant conversation you could say, has started. The resistance of the patient could be detected only in one or two comments, since I, as a psychologist, was obviously against his actual suicidal urges.	
Our cooperation lasted through the rehabilitation period. It was comprised of six sessions, several of which were hypnosis, mainly directed at soothing the pain in his leg on the same side of his amputated arm.	

Initial situation	Goal
– Reserved and hostile patient – Supposedly with all negative feelings (frustration, disappointment, pain, and hopelessness)	– Establishing connection and cooperation – Future orientation and motivation

DESCRIBER OF THE CASE: Katalin Varga, Psychologist.

THE FIRST EDITION: Varga K., Diószeghy Cs. (2001) *Hűtésbefizetés, avagy a szuggesztiók szerepe a mindennapi orvosi gyakorlatban.* /Cooling fee, or suggestions' role in the everyday medical practice/ Pólya Kiadó, Budapest, 49. oldal.

The Right Side

Original story	Note
Having come out of a coma following a brain varicose vein thrombosis, the young man is already on his way to recovery. This is not the first time I have visited him. He has been very unwell during the recent couple of hours. He looks scared. His body is now trembling, he is sweating, his right arm is tensed into a knot, and his pulse is 220 beats per minute (bpm). In his left hand, there is a 'spiky' ball he keeps rubbing against his chest. His skin is already red with irritation because of it.	The current situation is undoubtedly negative trance. However, the specialist can build on the previous relationship between the two of them. Stop it! You have a wound on your chest!
I'm standing on the patient's right side and his best friend is on the left. As I take over the rapport from the friend, I say to the patient over and over: *P.* (his friend's first name as the patient calls him) is *standing on your left side, and I'm on your right. You can hear my voice from the right, and his from the left... etc.*	Taking up rapport (in this case taking it over from the friend) begins with the description of the current (physical) orientation. The specialist associates herself consciously with the patient's friend. The above also serves as a multi-element **yes-set**.
In the meantime, I'm starting to softly stroke his tense right arm. "*Now your hand is shaking... you must feel a little vibration in it... this is a sign that you've begun to move your right side... This is going to be all right here too... from day to day you will be able to move your right hand more and more.*	**Rapport** is strengthened by soft stroking. The hand contact serves as a new element in the **yes-set** started earlier. The words used defuse the unpleasant symptoms (shaking, instead of cramping, **reframing**). The double meaning of the word 'right' provides an opportunity to further lead the patient's attention. The specialist attempts to dismiss unpleasant symptoms; she replaces tension and pain of the arm with positive associations (right). The unpleasant cramp receives a meaning as the sign of recovery (**reframing, future orientation**).

Original story	Note
In the meantime, (in about five to ten minutes) the patient visibly relaxes. He calms down, his facial features smooth out, he closes his eyes, and his pulse decreases to 83 bpm. In this state, we continue with general suggestions to support recovery.	The effectiveness of suggestions can also be followed on the monitor.

Initial situation	Goal
– Negative trance – Possible restlessness, pain, physical, and emotional distress – Physiological parameters corresponding to visual observation	– Dismiss negative trance and then turn it into positive trance – Relaxation, physically and emotionally, and positively reframing the symptom.

DESCRIBER OF THE CASE: Katalin Varga, Psychologist.

THE FIRST EDITION: Varga K., Diószeghy Cs. (2001) *Hűtésbefizetés, avagy a szuggesztiók szerepe a mindennapi orvosi gyakorlatban.* /Cooling fee, or suggestions' role in the everyday medical practice/ Pólya Kiadó, Budapest, 49. oldal.

Streptococcus

Original story	Note
Once during the night rounds I heard from the nurses that one of the mothers of the babies born that afternoon will not allow the start of the antibiotic treatment that was ordered by protocol. I asked the mother on the phone to come to my office for an examination with the newborn baby.	
During the course of the examination, I found everything to be all right. The baby was mature, healthy, and well developed. I shared my opinion with the mother.	Although the expert knows that the mother does not agree with the antibiotic treatment, she does not start with that topic. She builds the **rapport** with a common discussion of the positive results of the examination.
The examination included the Apgar test as well. The mother had earlier refused to have it done in the delivery room. I explained to her: *"We need to do this because this is the way we can get information about the integrity and penetrability of the nasal canal, the penetrability of the esophagus and its connection to the stomach, and the integrity and penetrability of the anus."* I showed her the thin, soft, and flexible plastic pipe we would use together to carry out the test carefully and without causing any discomfort to the baby. She agreed to the procedure, while she made sure that we did not cause any pain to the baby.	Before the 'main' question (the antibiotics), there is another hitch: the test. The mother now agrees to the procedure after simple (but positive) **information.** An important component of the information is the demonstration of the plastic probe (**object suggestion**). The examination with the mother's active participation gives her the feeling of control (**giving a sense of control**). She can now be sure that the procedure does not cause pain to her baby.

Original story	**Note**
Then I told her: *"The protocol of antibiotic treatment for newborns is based on decades of experience and research. The Streptococcus Class B is a pathogen that is absolutely harmless in adulthood but it can cause a very serious and fast process infection in newborn babies. In this case, they were lucky enough to deliver the baby girl so fast that there was no time for the administration of two doses of antibiotics beforehand.* *I suggested that we should not risk the infection now. Moreover, the antibiotics treatment does not cause significant pain or inconvenience to the baby. I could install a small canule into her hand with a small puncture (a lot of babies do not cry during the procedure) and through that we could inject the antibiotics without any pain. It is likely the baby will sleep through the procedure. If no pathogen grows from the sample taken from her ears, only four doses are needed. In case the treatment is extended to five days and you want to go home earlier, the last doses can be given orally at home."*	Then we had to turn to the necessity of the antibiotics. Again, the major element is factual information (**informing**). Observe: – At first, the doctor refers to professional experiences – The unfavourable outcome (serious infection) is not connected with this newborn baby but is anticipated generally Do you want your child to get a serious infection?? – She does not blame the mother for the absence of the former intake of antibiotics, but binds it to the lucky, fast progress of the delivery (now this is connected at present to the mother herself) – At the end of the information, she starts to 'gently' detail the procedure, finishing with the anticipation of the alternative treatment at home (**double-bind**).
I offered her that she could stay with the baby all along while I installed the canule.	With the new alternative (**double-bind**), the mother gets to experience the feeling of being in control (staying together with the child or not).

Original story	Note
She was happy to see (I admit, so was I) that the canule could be installed without the baby crying. Moreover, now we could take reliable measurements of the baby's blood-sugar level through the canule to monitor the baby's good adaption to extra-uterine life.	The good blood sugar level measured in connection with the installation of the canule is another positive fact, just like the opening of the whole situation. Therefore, the procedure is placed in this positive 'sandwich'.
The mother brought her child with a smile to the antibiotics treatment twice a day and after the little girl's outer ear canal culture, they stayed in the neonatal department until the end of the treatment.	Based on proper information, good cooperation develops.

Initial situation	Goal
– A mother disapproving of a procedure	– To convince the mother and accomplish the procedure with her approval

DESCRIBER OF THE CASE: Olga Kónyi Dr., Neonatologist.

THE FIRST EDITION: Exam paper for the postgraduate training program on Suggestive Communication in Somatic Medicine, co-organised by the Hungarian Association of Hypnosis and Semmelweis University School of Medicine, Budapest.

Maybe We'll Meet Again…

Original story	Note
A woman with eyes red from crying came to the gynecology check-in desk. With her ultrasound (US) papers (medical records) in her hands, she told me that she was Magdolna Sz., in her 36th week of gestation, and that she was here for admittance. There was no longer any fetal heartbeat.	
We generally admit patients at the nurses' desk, but in this case, I myself showed her and her husband to her room and I let them withdraw. (Fortunately, we did have a room with both beds vacant.) She changed into hospital garb and she said goodbye to her husband who had to go pick up their son.	Providing a more intimate atmosphere in this situation and carrying on with the admittance procedure into a room with privacy deviates from the usual routine, but it certainly is a nice gesture.
I sat down next to her bed and we started talking about things beyond the official admittance routine. The conversation was halted from time to time by her inconsistent use of first name terms.	In Hungarian, the agreement on being formal or being on a first name basis is a good starting point for **establishing rapport**.
From her anamnesis, I already knew that Magdolna had a caesarean two years ago. She told me that her little son was very much looking forward to his new baby sibling. She couldn't imagine how she would tell him what even she herself had not been able to really grasp yet. She told me that she had still felt her baby move just the previous day, but in the US that day they did not detect the heartbeat.	

Original story	Note
During our conversation, she mentioned several times that she did not want to cry. I reassured her that she could cry. Then, clinging to my arms, she wept and wept. It was hard not to say a word during this episode. Eventually, as a result of sheer exhaustion, she could sleep for a couple of hours.	In the difficult situation, crying is appropriate, especially if the person is in the hands of a professional who is able to take it in and can follow it. In the case of acute losses, nothing really has to be said and the most (and very important!) a professional can do is to support the involved persons in letting out their emotions.
She was hoping "to get over the whole thing" as soon as possible and it was hard for her to accept the doctors' decision to wait and see if labour would start naturally. I sat beside her bed again, and we talked, or rather, I was a listener while she contemplated; sometimes I nodded in approval and sometimes I asked a few questions here and there.	Seemingly, it would really be easier to be over with everything in a short time. However, in the long run, those who do not forgo facing the difficult situation, experiencing the emotions belonging here, come off better. An attentive and empathic professional is of great help.
At last she came to the conclusion that since things had turned out this way, she would use this time to say goodbye to her baby daughter and to figure out what to tell the little boy.	In case of every loss, be it a dead person or the loss of a limb or an organ, it helps to move on if we can say goodbye to it. No matter how young a child is, it is advisable to reveal the truth in an objective manner. Being secretive and blurring the issue merely increases the child's loneliness and confusion. As from his parents' behaviour (or in this case from the absence of the baby sibling), he will know that something is wrong.
Before I left her, I mentioned that she might want to consider if she or they both wanted to see their baby after her birth. I didn't expect an answer. I simply brought up the issue for her to consider and to be prepared for. (Only between brackets: I also thought that she might not even be asked, and later when there would no longer be any chance to choose, they would feel the need.)	The question is not only of practical use (though the issue really may come up unexpectedly immediately after the birth of the baby, and thus it is not sure they could give an adequately considered response). In this case, this question could help deepen the experience of losing the baby, accept the loss, and what is more, it offers a forward perspective through its **future orientation**.

Original story	Note
I didn't expect an answer, but amid vehement objection she said, "no, no, no way." *"Alright,"* I said, and promised to come in to see her tomorrow.	In spite of the fact that the professional does not agree with the mother's decision, she respects it (**giving a sense of control**). Referring to them seeing each other the following day, besides maintaining the **rapport,** also strengthens the **future orientation.**
The following afternoon, I went to the hospital and the first thing I did was to ask my colleagues if anything had happened. "Nothing," was the answer.	
As I entered the room, Magdolna seemed very excited and she immediately bombarded me with her questions: "Why did you tell me to decide whether I wanted to see her? I was thinking about this the whole night. I have never seen a dead human. What does a dead baby look like? Would you look at her? I am afraid to look at her, and anyway, I thought I would never see her…ever."	The suggestion made by the professional the previous day has been brewing in the mother's mind…
Suddenly, I didn't know which question to answer first, so I referred back to the last one: *"And what do you think now?"* "I don't know. This is why I was waiting for you! What does a dead baby look like?" *"It is almost like a live one,"* I replied "As if she was sleeping?" *"Yes."* "I don't know… I'd like to see her, but… I am afraid…"	The ambivalence is clear. However, it is not the professional who has to solve the situation. She supports the mother in finding her *own* decision.

Original story	Note
"Why would it be good for you to see her? "I'd see what she is like……. I am curious to see what she would have been like…..," she cried. *"Why would it be good to see what she looks like?"* "That's somehow more real…. I would have something to remember….," she cried, and I did not think that it would be a good idea to say anything.	The professional's questions that resonate with **positivity** (!) (why would it be good?) are more times based on the mother's words (**repetition**).
Before I left the room, she asked for my phone number. I gave it to her and promised that on the following day when I worked in the delivery room, that I would come over to see her as soon as I had some time.	The mother initiates an ever deeper relationship with the professional. This is natural. Moreover, it is a step that sheds a favourable light on the cooperation so far. However, we must be aware if it approaches an uncomfortable level for us.
On the third day in the morning, I started my shift in the delivery room. Magdolna came over that morning, as it seemed that labour had started. It was natural for me that I would be with them. She had irregular contractions, she was one finger (less than one centimeter) dilated. After the rupture of the membranes, we waited for her contractions to get more regular.	Waiting for days, according to the above said, can be the time that supports the acceptance of the situation and the loss. It is no use hastening it (not even for psychological reasons), if it is possible.
When I had time, I went in to check on them. Magdolna brought the issue of seeing the baby again. Her husband wouldn't, but she decided to see her. I was happy with her decision.	It took her days to reach the decision. But this way, it was based on sufficient consideration.

Original story	Note
I had a lot to do and could not be with them all the time, but I felt it was better this way. Magdolna seemed quite calm, but her husband was very nervous, just like he was two days before. I thought it was better for them to be by themselves.	
Meanwhile time was going by, but the birth would not proceed. Magdolna's husband started to become more relaxed and one time he came out after me. He too wanted to know if it is a good idea that they see the baby. I assured him that I support both of them in their own decisions and if his wife wants to see the baby, I'll show the baby to her and if he is unsure then I won't show the baby to him. I saw that he was very uncertain about his decision, and he also told me that he was confused. From one moment to another, he had to accept that he would not have a second child and that the dream day that they were hoping for eight months were now shattered. It had not even occurred to him that the baby could be looked at after birth and now he did not know what to do… I assured him that he still had some time to decide what he would like to do. I suggested that he should think over what the most helpful scenario would be to help accept all of those things that he was talking about. He went back to the delivery room with tears in his eyes.	The professional now supports the father with her accepting attitude. In line with the good **rapport** formed with the mother, the trust relationship has good bases. Notice that the professional neither hastens the father, nor does she decide for him, even in this case when the mother has already decided to see the baby.

Original story	Note
In the afternoon, as the birth did not proceed, Magdolna's doctor decided on a caesarean section. I prepared her, and before entering the operating room, they asked me when and how they could see their baby girl together after the surgery. We agreed that before she was taken to her room, they would have a chance to see their baby girl.	
Magdolna entered the operating room and her husband was weeping, sunken into the small bench in the waiting room. I stayed with him as long as I could.	Amidst the father's "doing nothing", the emotional support from the midwife is a particularly nice gesture.
Then I went into the operating room for the baby, whom I brought out wrapped in sheets, holding her closely. Up until this moment, I managed to contain myself quite well, but now that I stayed alone with the baby my tears started to fall. I washed her, wiped her, and measured her. Her tiny body had been macerated almost everywhere, but I hoped that I can manage to wrap her in a sheet so that only her little face could be seen.	The emotional involvement of the midwife is understandable. Luckily she also leaves space for it.
When Magdolna was wheeled out of the operating room, I accompanied her husband into the hallway and then I brought in the baby. I would have liked to leave them alone in order to let them be able to say goodbye to their baby "without an audience", but I could not place her little body anywhere adequate where Magdolna could see her from the stretcher, and I was also concerned that my careful wrapping would open up. So, I held her in my arms when her parents looked at her, both smiling and crying.	The motivation to bring home a nice visual memory of their lost baby daughter with them cements the situation: the midwife also stays with the parents in spite of the fact that she may have exposed them to further extreme emotional stress.

Original story	Note
"Beautiful," they said, and they both caressed her little face. (I must admit that I cried as well, though I knew I should not have let myself do this.)	There is a place for the emotions of the professional.
Magdolna was taken back to the gynaecology ward. By now, the second bed had been filled. So we moved her to a single room where her husband could stay with her without disturbing anyone and without being disturbed.	
Around midday on the fourth day around, I visited Magdolna at the hospital. She moved around surprisingly well, as if she had not even had a caesarean section. She had a vague smile on her face as she talked about how beautiful her late daughter was and how much she resembled their little boy. She added that they had decided to tell their son everything. She was very eager to go home to see him.	Positive signs in the mother: good post-op condition, slight smile, and the decision is made to tell everything to the son. All this suggests that she is on the right track regarding mourning and letting go.
On the tenth day, Magdolna called me to ask if I thought there was still a chance to ask for the body of their baby daughter. We both knew that it might be too late but it was worth a try. They had decided they would like to bury her. I told her where to ask for the information and I kept my fingers crossed.	

Original story	Note
On the 14th day, I received an e-mail: Dear Gabi, Guess what: we have managed to arrange the funeral. I don't know if it will be better for us, but at least her little body does not just get thrown out and we'll have a place to go to remember. The result of the post-mortem is: multiple spread placenta necroses. My poor little one, maybe she was completely healthy... We would have named her Anna. Fortunately, we still have Adam, who gives us lots of joy. And Zsolt is also beside me and it means so much. I'm also attaching a photo of our beautiful little boy and we are sending lots of hugs to you. I cannot be thankful enough for what you have done for us and the way you helped us. Maybe we'll see each other again... Magdi, Ádám, Zsolt I was very happy with the "Maybe we'll see each other again..." sentence, as Magdolna told me several times that it is good that she already has a child because after this she would not dare think of having another baby again...	The future orientation reached its goal: at the moment as a vague suggestion, but the idea of a new baby is articulated...

Initial situation	Goal
– Negative trance because of the acute loss	– Emotional support – Helping the acceptance of loss – Starting the mourning work

DESCRIBER OF THE CASE: Gabriella Vass, Midwife.

THE FIRST EDITION: Exam paper for the postgraduate training program on Suggestive Communication in Somatic Medicine, co-organised by the Hungarian Association of Hypnosis and Semmelweis University School of Medicine, Budapest.

Old Lady With a Bunch of Flowers

Original story	Note
The doctor of an old lady asked me to have a word with her patient for she was refusing to eat, exercise, and cooperate with anyone at all. She was just lying there with her eyes closed and she kept repeating that all she wanted to do was die. This was the full extent of her communication to the world.	
The lady lies in the intensive care unit with her eyes closed, looking rather grumpy when I arrive. But in fact, this attitude is almost of her crying for help: 'Hey, notice me! Interact with me!' She only has her eyes closed when there surely is someone watching her. She pretends not to notice that I'm standing next to her bed and that I want her attention. The attention would evidently be of no value if she gave it to anyone just like that. But now, someone is finally here, asking for a little contact. However, I do not buy into her fine hysterics. Therefore, she simply 'has to' talk to me. She conveys that all she wants is to die and that she is no longer interested in anything whatsoever.	Carefully observing the patient's behaviour is the first step towards **building rapport.** The psychologist uses a little 'rigorous' pressure to establish contact with the patient. The result: it turns out that in the complete lack of motivation to live, the patient has rejected the option for recovery.
Then it turns out that her family does not visit her anymore, which she feels she deserves. The nurses disagree with this, asserting that visitors are not allowed in the hospital at the moment due to the influenza epidemic. But she does not believe this.	The visitors are also drawn under the effect of negative trance.

Original story	**Note**
She is, by the way, 80 years old and has no reason to live. Her time is up. If Death comes and grabs her hand, she will go along. "*Of course, when it is time, well, we all have to go,*" I say and she nods in response. But she cannot resist to see if I am out of my mind. Of course I am.	Don't be so silly! The specialist conveys her agreement with an undeniable statement (if it is time, we have to go) which comes through as quite surprising in the present situation. This awakens curiosity in the patient and it deepens the **rapport**.
So we keep talking. "*I'm not saying either that we can plan for another 20 years.*" Then I draft the goal; to get off the machine, take the drain out, leave the unit, and get home.	Realistic goal setting is the basis of **cooperation**. Pacing turns into slight **leading**.
But she does not want to go home because the family does not deserve it. Besides, she is already old and she'd rather die here.	Unfortunately, the patient is unmotivated for the future goals, especially for going home.
"*Well, you* will *die one day, that's for sure. And this is not going to be in 20 years' time. But not now either. And well, it does matter how you feel until then. If the family does not deserve you at home, then you don't deserve to suffer for them. However, you do deserve to get better and be more comfortable, don't you? It is surely more comfortable without the machine. You are progressing nicely towards this goal but your cooperation is needed too.*"	The specialist builds again on the undeniable statement of 'you will die one day'. However, following this, she immediately confidently states: 'not now' (**direct suggestion**). Rearranging the elements of the relationship with the family, she says that the patient does not deserve to suffer. The direct and hard-to-deny fact of the comfort provided by the lack of machine/drain takes over the previous plans regarding the future (**goal centering**). The specialist calls upon cooperation (**direct suggestion**).

Original story	Note
She waves her hand; what for, she will shortly die. *"Well yes, but until then... it is better to die without a drain."* This is undeniable to such an extent that it is now easy to draft the recovery process now that we have a goal: to die without a drain. The lady is now open to hear what she needs to do.	The specialist meets the patient on the field of the undeniable statement of 'It is better to die without a drain'. This, they both agree with and so they unite in this goal.
In the next day or two, she eats properly, sits outside, and sometimes I talk to her to help the process. Talking is especially useful when they take the stoma out, then eventually must put back. I have to tell to her that it is alright and that it is indeed taken out. In the meantime she is isolated for a while because of an infection.	Following the previously established **rapport** and the commonly accepted goal, it is enough to make contact with the patient only time to time. Especially at the (real or imagined) sensitive periods following treatment.
One day the nurses tell me that there is something wrong with the lady because she is just lying in bed all day with her eyes closed. I don't know if she can recognise me in the mask or not. But she smiles at me: 'Are you here again?' then she closes her eyes again. "It is so beautiful!" *"What is beautiful?"* "Beautiful." *"But what?"* Then it turns out that when she closes her eyes, she sees all kind of beautiful things. Memories, maybe things that have not even happened yet. Landscapes that are so good to look at.	The patient feels comfortable to share her fantasies/daydreaming/hallucinations with the psychologist based on their existing relationship. The psychologist welcomes the images. What seemed to be depressive passivity turns out to be a pleasant period of floating dreams. This became quickly evident after having established the appropriate relationship.

Original story	Note
"*What do you see now?*" "I see flowers. A big, field of flowers. Small, big, colourful. And there are children too – they are running up and down," she smiles. They can be seen even when she opens her eyes and she shows them to me. I also learn that it brings her peace and pleasure as she watches these images. She finds her peace in them. She feels good. She had a dream last night about the cemetery. She was lying on the ground in a black dress. Her skin was white and cold, and rain was falling on her. "It was very bad. Then I got lost in the street and that boy came," she points at a junior doctor, "he grabbed my hand and showed me home."	The new question leads the psychologist further into the patient's inner world till the dream in which she meets Death.
I am amazed. I suddenly remember that just the other day a guy talked about the erotic death images of the Etruscans. They believed that Death comes in the form of a seducer of the opposite sex and leads people away. Is she already preparing to die? If she does, she does it beautifully. But the cemetery was not good, she only feels comfortable among these flowery images. It turns out we are not dying here yet.	A not-so-rare synchronicity…. The specialist has to pay attention to her own emotional involvement in such cases… If one manages to get 'asked into' an old, close-to-death patient's world, then one has to stand to what awaits there.
In order to add something to Life, I tell her how beautiful the snowdrops were that I saw in the forest. She looks at me strictly: 'You mustn't pick those!' "I didn't touch them, I only took a picture of them". She nods relieved. Then she looks at me and laughs, "You saw flowers too."	Alongside the world of fantasies and dreams, appears the motif of reality (**reality orientation, metaphors**). The trustful relationship, positive attuning of the elderly patient and young psychologist, becomes clearer and clearer.

Original story	Note
Two to three weeks later, I am told that the lady was seen walking by herself on the general medicine unit. What could she have found that she judged as worth completing before she dies?	

Initial situation	Goal
– Depressive and passive patient	– Cooperation and establishing a trustful relationship – Awake motivation for recovery

DESCRIBER OF THE CASE: Adrienn K. Szilágyi, Clinical Psychologist.

THE FIRST EDITION: Case report to this volume.

Femoral Fracture

Original story	Note
Unfortunately, the system in our hospital is such that it is only before the operation that we, anaesthesiologists, meet our patient to anaesthetise and narcotise them. One day, an 83-year-old lady who had to be operated on due to a femoral fracture, arrived at my theatre. She had been examined the day before and the doctor thought that I should decide which anaesthetic method to use, depending on her current state. However, the patient had many co-morbid disorders, and according to my judgement, she was in such a state that the operation could only be performed if it was vital. A femoral fracture is not such an urgent condition. I discussed the issue with the surgeons, who said they should definitely operate. If I decided not to anaesthetise her myself, then they would do it themselves locally, and so they did. I thought I had nothing to lose, so why not try the 'favourite place' suggestion during the operation, since I know from experience that local anaesthetics will not be sufficient for this kind of intervention. They are unable to infiltrate the most profound layers. Besides, repositioning the fracture will inevitably cause pain.	

Original story	**Note**
"Aunty Lisbett! (she has allowed me to call her so) *You are going to have an operation now under anaesthetics. The doctor who will do your operation will give an injection in your leg where it has broken. In your hip. I am going to be here with you throughout. If you have any complaint, please feel free to tell me. In the meantime, we can talk about anything else. Can you recall any pleasant memories? Perhaps a place where you felt good?"* "No, I can't." *"Is there nothing you recall with pleasant feelings? Anything? A place or a person?"* "No, nothing." *"Nobody? Children perhaps?"* "I do have children but I haven't heard from them for a long time." *"Do you like the beach or lake Balaton perhaps?"* "No."	In this situation, the anaesthesiologist practically has no choice: the doctors' choice and judgement disagrees with hers. The first thing to note is that she leaves her anxiety unrevealed in front of the patient (let alone share it with her), but accepts the situation and will be present for the procedure. The patient is **informed** in a both factual and **positive** way: she does not emphasise what *could* be, but rather what is *going to be.* In this situation, it can be especially disturbing that the patient refuses to cooperate despite the supportive attitude and informing from the anaesthesiologist.

Original story	Note
In the meantime, while we struggled to find a pleasant memory in her life, we had arrived at the first painful stage, repositioning the fracture. This was preceded by the anaesthetic injection. *"Now you are going to feel a little puncture in your hip which is the anaesthetic injection. As we inject it, you are going to feel a pleasant, tingling sensation where there was pain before. Can you feel it?"* "Yes I can." *"What kind of sensation is this?"* "Nice and cool."	The anaesthesiologist immediately links the expected feelings due to the intervention with pleasant sensations: puncture, anaesthetic, previous pain, and tingling sensation (**reframing**). Note that despite previous experiences with the colleagues, the anaesthesiologist remains in-group with them ('we inject'). This is when the first positive answer arrives, describing the sensation as 'nice and cool'.
"Stay focused on this cool feeling as it expands. Let it expand… And as it expands, the previously unpleasant sensation will go away as well." "I can feel something very pleasant and cool." *"Good, this cool sensation will accompany you during the operation."* In the meantime the operation has begun.	This nice and cool feeling is linked with the distancing of the previously unpleasant sensations (**pacing-leading**). Since the anaesthesiologist receives additional positive feedback from the patient, the positive effect can be expanded to the whole period of the operation (**future orientation**).
"You may feel a little 'bucking' in the cool area. The operation has begun and so has the recovery. How do you feel?" "Good, thank you."	The experience of the operation is described as 'bucking' (**reframing**). Then comes another foreseeing perspective: the recovery has begun (**future orientation**). The patient's experience remains pleasant.

Original story	Note
"Great, in this case, in order to facilitate even more in the recovery process, we are going to perform a breathing exercise." The patient is severely asthmatic. *"Take a slow deep breath… like that… now exhale slowly… good… Inhale again and when you exhale, you can feel as if the fresh air pervades your body all the way to your bones… until it reaches the fractured bone… like that… once more, nice and slowly… Now you keep breathing slowly but freely… Can you feel as the fresh air pervades your body?"* "Yes I can."	The following suggestions stress even further the process of recovery (**implication**) mentioned before. To do this, we will perform a simple breathing exercise (**direct suggestion**). Note the anaesthesiologist's use of the wording of **cooperation** ('we are going to perform'). The fresh air that she breathes in serves to heal the fractured bones (**repetition**). In addition to this, she responds positively to the specialists question; the fresh air pervades her whole body. By asking a series of questions, the anaesthesiologist maintains the interaction, which is accompanied by the positive and reinforcing answers of the patient (**maintaining rapport**).
"How do you feel?" "It hurts a little by my femoral." *"What else do you feel apart from the pain?"* "I feel something cool there." *"Good… perhaps this coolness will soon reach the place of puncture as well."*	Following the first unpleasant sign (hurts a little), the doctor immediately distracts the patient a little by asking *what else* she feels. To the coolness she responds by encouraging the spreading of this sensation: up until the place of the puncture.

Original story	Note
It was not long now until the end of the operation: only the closure of the wound remained. *"Soon the operation ends and your fractured femoral is in place. Your hip is stable now; you will soon be able to lift your leg again. This cool sensation will stay by the hip for a while, then it will slowly disappear. Until the sensation leaves, however, it will help you recover."*	At the end of the operation, the patient again receives information about what is happening (**informing**). Starting with the actual problem (fractured femoral), through to the solution (it is fixed, stable), and up until good functioning (you will be able to lift it again), they advance gradually. In the process, the well-known 'cool feeling' returns again, further facilitating recovery.
Overall in this case, the patient did not complain of significant pain and the operation could therefore happen. Local anaesthetising has probably succeeded exceptionally well too. However, she has definitely received mental support and benefited from breathing exercises.	

Initial situation	Goal
– The anaesthesiologist has remained alone with her professional views – Patient who refuses to cooperate at the beginning	– To ensure the maximum possible comfort during the operation

DESCRIBER OF THE CASE: Gabriella Kovács Dr., Anesthesiologist, Intensive Care Specialist.

THE FIRST EDITION: Exam paper for the postgraduate training program on Suggestive Communication in Somatic Medicine, co-organised by the Hungarian Association of Hypnosis and Semmelweis University School of Medicine, Budapest.

Dental Plaque

Original story	Note
A 38-year-old man arrives at the dentist's office.	
We introduce ourselves. He says that all his teeth hurt. During anamnesis, his mind wanders off: '*I have had enough of everything anyway, my teeth hurt and my girlfriend has left me.*' He is sad and depressed. When I check his teeth, the picture of a much neglected and full-of-plaque mouth strikes me.	What is really interesting in this story is the dilemma of whether or not the doctor should deal with the patient's private issues he initially brings up. You really neglected your teeth!
"Plaque often causes a sensation as if all your teeth hurt," I inform him. *"It can simply be removed and the uncomfortable feeling is gone."* He consents. We start the treatment. Not so keenly, but he opens his mouth.	At first sight, the information regarding the plaque (**informing, positivity**) can easily be transferred to the man's current situation (**future orientation**).
"Perhaps you can feel as if your teeth break free and are almost reborn... It will feel good to touch them with your tongue. You will be able to feel the clean and smooth surface of your teeth and the soft and healthy surface of the gums." The patient already paws his teeth in the pause of the treatment.	The two-level communication is further continued. It can be applied to the current life situation as well: break free, reborn, feels good, clean, healthy, etc. (**positivity, future orientation**)
"And perhaps it will feel good that a man like you, who is living one of the best times of his life, will now smile more bravely and happily with his new, white, and shiny teeth... and this can positively influence your environment and your relationships. You surely know that this enjoyable state can be maintained with a little care and attention, like many other things in life."	The achievable successes of the future are referred to by the doctor (**future orientation, positivity**). Referring to 'one of the best times of a man's life' **implies** that there will be other good times. This further strengthens the general picture of the future, which has started with the plaque.

Original story	Note
"I'll show you a couple of moves that can make your oral hygiene practices more effective. I'll also recommend a plaque-fighting toothpaste." The patient is relaxed and actively repeats the movements I showed him with a toothbrush in his hand.	Practical advice (**informing**).
"Very good. I can see that you are doing it better and better... I would like to see you again in two to three days to check on your healthy gums and shiny teeth."	Asking him to come back is tentative enough and it is the man's own decision whether or not he returns. The time frame is large enough to provide a **sense of control**. The goal is confidently pronounced (healthy gum and shiny teeth) (**direct suggestion, future orientation**).
He comes back again two months later. He is of good humour and smiling broadly. He tells me that he is in a new relationship now and that he is happy. And by the way, he showed his new girlfriend the 'tricks' of tooth-brushing.	

Initial situation	Goal
– Sad and depressed patient – Neglected mouth	– Cheer him up, in addition to the usual treatment – Motivation to use proper oral-hygiene.

DESCRIBER OF THE CASE: Varga Krisztina Dr., Dentist.

THE FIRST EDITION: Exam paper for the postgraduate training program on Suggestive Communication in Somatic Medicine, co-organised by the Hungarian Association of Hypnosis and Semmelweis University School of Medicine, Budapest.

Blood for Sale

Original story	Note
The Intensive Care Unit asked for psychological consultation in the treatment of a 24-year-old young man suffering from Guillain-Barre syndrome[1]. According to the Unit, the patient suffered from depression and could not cope with immobility, assisted breathing, speechlessness, and helplessness. I saw him every other day and we prepared tapes for the time in between. One day, his family met me with great agitation. They told me that the client was planning to leave the hospital, abandoning his treatment.	
When I arrived at his bed, the exhausted man whispered to me: "They want to kill me. Take me away from here! They suck my blood and sell it abroad." I was shocked to see him in this speechless and immobile state, helplessly floundering in his bed.	The reality orientation of the young man is biased just as any other person's in a similar situation would be. He is a good example of someone in a 'paranoid work state'. Obviously his concern is based on a misunderstanding – he could have misheard or dreamt something, or both. Instead of being thankful you are indicting us!
Then I asked why he thought that was so.	Building on our previously developed good **rapport,** I accepted what he said. I did this as the first step towards the solution (**pacing-**) instead of trying to convince him otherwise.

1 This is an autoimmune disorder which quickly results in paralysis (including respiratory muscles). This happens with the patient's full awareness as the normal state of mind is intact.

Original story	Note
He 'told me' that too much blood is drawn from him and he heard that they are planning to sell it abroad.	My inquiry provides him with an opportunity to tell me the details. This might seem as the opposite of what we are trying to achieve here, but in fact, this gives him the feeling that he is being listened to and taken seriously (**pacing**).
I took his complaint seriously. I told him that I think this is very unlikely to be true because I know the hospital staff very well. In addition to this, I commented, "*his blood is not of good quality which is the very reason it is being cleaned.*"	A psychologist not formally attached to the Unit can be a good 'mediator'. Protection of the client is just as important to the mediator as it is to the interest of the hospital. The first reaction of the specialist touches on the fact that his assumption is incorrect (**strengthening reality orientation**). At the same time, he is 'reminded' that he is here as a patient needing treatment. This is the first vague step towards **leading:** he has to stay here and undergo treatment.
We agreed that I would check on what was happening to him, after which we would make any decisions. He agreed.	What was 'his problem' before now becomes 'our problem' (**cooperation**). We state that we would make any decision *together*.
I asked his doctor why and when his blood is drawn. They explained everything to me and showed me the tubes and medical charts. Indeed, a lot of tests were being done in addition to the usual routine tests: there were many additional blood tests due to his illness. I took all these back to the patient, explaining him the situation in detail.	The specialist **informs him** of the information received directly from the doctor. The objects serve as proof that the enquiry had indeed taken place (**object suggestions**) and at the same time, they function as a rational explanation of why so much blood needed to be drawn (**recovery of reality orientation**).

Original story	Note
As I spoke, he became calmer and calmer. *"So do you understand why now?"* "Yes." *"Do you see why your blood needs to be constantly drawn?"* "Yes." *"Is the situation any easier to bear now?"* "Yes." *"Will you stay?"* "Yes." *"So the treatment can continue, can't it?"* "Yes it can."	Sharing of information which ends as a **yes-set.** At the end, we make the patient pronounce that he is willing to stay in the hospital and undergo the treatment (this was the basis of the initial complaint).
Then we called in his wife and mother in front of whom we repeated the conversation. He also told them that the situation is now clear and he wants further treatment.	Sharing the outcome with the family provides a good opportunity to **repeat** the steps above, as well as reassure them, since the last time they saw the man he was very agitated.
Because, according to him, the outcome was 'too good', I told him as I was saying goodbye that if he had any queries in the future, he should clarify it with the staff: *"Please feel free to ask any questions from who you feel you can trust the most, should it be the nurse, doctor, or me and we will find answers for you."*	The format 'question or query' weakens the edge of the current, desperately mistrustful situation (**reframing**). Closing offers a wide range of specialists who, regardless of his choice, will provide a reassuring answer to his query (**double-bind**). This is regarding the current as well as future situations (**future orientation**).

Initial situation	Goal
– Exhausted and desperate client (and family) – Negative trance, paranoid work state	– Breaking of the negative trance and recovery of reality orientation. – (Re-)building of trust with staff

DESCRIBER OF THE CASE: Katalin Varga, Psychologist.

THE FIRST EDITION: Varga K. (2005) *Szuggesztív kommunikáció a szomatikus orvoslásban.* /Suggestive communication in somatic medication/ Országos Addiktológiai Intézet, Budapest. pp. 420–433.

Flyboy

Original story	Note
A middle-aged man makes an appointment for dental treatment. His speech is fast and excited. He reports that one of his friends, who had been very satisfied with the treatment he had received here not long ago, recommended them.	
The patient appears at the prearranged time. He is noticeably very tense. He is sweating and his face is red. I introduce myself and we sit down for a while in the waiting room. We exchange a few words about his friend. I bring up how happy his friend was with the reconstruction of his teeth.	The patient shows the signs of negative trance. The dentist goes out to the waiting room and she waits for her next patient (**pacing**). The introduction further supports the rapport, which, in this case, starts from a good basis because of the recommendation of a friend. The doctor turns it to good use and recalls the happiness caused by the reconstruction of the teeth. All of this is obviously valid in the present too (**goal centering, future orientation, modeling**).
"Would you accompany me to my office?" I ask him wickedly as some acknowledgement of his strong masculine role.	The 'luscious' gesture nearly forces the patient to put away his fear and reluctance. It would be really difficult to reject this request.
He is still extremely nervous in the dental chair. He tells me that after a bad experience he has not seen a dentist for eight years.	
"I understand that you are tense now, maybe afraid too… I wonder whether you have ever been similarly tense in a different life situation."	The doctor openly conceptualises the patient's negative emotions (**pacing, empathic answer**).
After a short consideration, he answers, "Yes, before takeoff, you know, flying is my hobby. That's where I get my adrenaline fix."	Perfect answer: the patient mentions a positive, voluntary life situation, drawing a parallel with the present treatment by himself (**modeling**: the patient can take himself as a model, in a different situation).

Original story	Note
"That could be fantastic!... As you are rising into the air, the tension gradually gives way to a state of peaceful calmness... You may find it interesting that while you're recalling these emotions, your facial features have become more relaxed." Indeed, the flush has disappeared from his face. His breathing has become calm and regular.	The doctor retunes the excitement to calmness in the frame of flying (**reframing**). Then, by concretising it to the present situation, she starts the relaxing suggestions (**leading**).
We discuss the steps and the possible achievements of the treatment (beautiful smile, joyful eating, relieved and happy laughing, etc.) and he leaves with a referral for an X-ray.	Besides the illustration of the steps of the treatment (**informing**), the detailed conceptualisation of the possible achievements is also important (**goal centering, future orientation, positivity**).
He arrives to the following appointment with a clumsy smile. Before and during the procedure, it is enough to refer to his hobby of flying with a few words and we can cooperate very well in the subsequent two hours. His face is calm and his breath is regular all the way through.	The rapport built at the previous meeting and the motif of flying (**repetition**) gives a proper background to the long-lasting treatment.
By the way, on every December 25th, I get Christmas greetings and a thank-you text message with the signature of 'the flyboy' Y.X.	

Initial situation	Goal
– Nervous, distrustful patient – Unpleasant previous experiences – Good model: recommendation from a friend	– Development of trust and cooperation – Development of physical and psychological relaxation

DESCRIBER OF THE CASE: Krisztina Varga Dr., Dentist.

THE FIRST EDITION: Exam paper for the postgraduate training program on Suggestive Communication in Somatic Medicine, co-organised by the Hungarian Association of Hypnosis and Semmelweis University School of Medicine, Budapest.

Next to Me...

Original story	Note
Zsanett is a 23-year-old, kind, smiling, and talkative young gipsy woman. She had been unsuccessfully trying to become pregnant for years. By this time, Zsanett and her partner have been medically checked from head to toe; however, no abnormalities were found. Luckily the situation had spontaneously changed. She was 32 weeks pregnant when we met. We met one day when I went downstairs to see a colleague as I had nothing to do in the acute labour room. It was late at night already but the corridor in front of the admission room was still noisy. I could hardly enter the corridor because of the crowd of people, which as I found out later, consisted of members of Zsanett's family. I could overhear when the doctor on duty informed the extended family about the necessary tests and planned treatment, and when he asked them to leave considering the later hour. Following a brief discussion, they had indeed left, since their loved one was now in good hands. "I am glad you are here!" said my colleague. This pregnant woman has just arrived. She is in her 32nd week and is having contractions. The doctor on duty ordered tocanisation[2] in the labour room in order to prevent premature birth. With these words, she entrusted the girl to me. Zsanett was scared, sad, and longed for her family.	

2 Used to medically stop contractions of the womb.

Original story	Note
After introducing myself, I told her that I am the one on duty in the labour room. Then referring to the doctor's order, I collected her belongings and put them all into a nylon bag. Then, I took her arm and accompanied her to the labour room.	The previous scene suggests that she is still in a deep emotional connection (**rapport**) with her family. This is especially important to note in order to take over the rapport successfully. Introduction, naming the goal, and the physical contact (taking her arm) serve this purpose. It should also be noted that the girl may be uncertain and distrusting as a result of her previously unsuccessful efforts to conceive.
Zsanett moved her legs slowly and was frightened as she walked up the stairs with me. If it was up to her, she would have turned back and ran after her family. She was unfamiliar with the hospital environment, the cleanness, the smell of the disinfectant, and the well coordinated work of the staff. As a result, she probably identified her time here with losing her freedom.	
Approaching the labour room door, I explained to her that she was very lucky as nobody is actually in labour so she can rest in a peaceful and calm environment while she is having the infusion therapy as prescribed. As a result of the therapy, the unpleasant contractions will disappear and the baby can develop without interruption until he/she is mature enough to come out.	The introduction to the new environment (**informing**) at the same time contains suggestions about the peaceful and calm environment (**implication**). The aim of the intervention is expressed on a personal level: 'the contractions will disappear and the baby can develop further' (**motivating**).
At this moment, we enter the door. I enthusiastically invite her to choose the room in which she would like to sit. I thought we would consider the possibilities together. She must like one or the other. According to my previous experience, soon to be moms appreciate this little gesture and are happy to choose. Some vote on a smaller, friendlier room, while others prefer larger spaces.	The possibility of choice (**double,** or in this case **multiple-bind**) provides a sense of **control** to the young lady. The midwife does all this routinely because she has direct experience on just how well it affects young moms and on how it improves the specialist's authenticity.

Original story	Note
I tell her happily about my experience that women in this state are especially good at detecting internal sensations.	Referring to the other women stands as a positive **model** for the young mom: what seemed to be her first and unique experience becomes a collective one. This may decrease her anxiety and loneliness.
Zsanett looks around the empty room. She stopped in front of a conventional hospital bed and asked anxiously: "Do I really have to lie here on my own?" *"I am also going to be here and near you"* I replied. Then she burst into a desperate cry.	The details of the place make the woman realise what awaits her…
Following constant asking, she finally admitted what is she is really feeling… "*I have never slept alone in a bed before! I am afraid that I won't be able to fall asleep unless someone sleeps next to me!*" she said. Well, this indeed seemed to be an irresolvable problem! I offered her the possibility to stay near her; however, I was unable to suggest staying physically close to her as a way of comforting her.	The need of the patient and the willingness of the specialist are not identical…

Original story	Note
I wanted to find a solution to win her cooperation as soon as possible. Then I thought of a technique I learned at the suggestive communication training (**yes-set**) and so I started. *"Zsanett, it has been a long time since you wanted a child, hasn't it?"* "Yes" she replied. *"The baby moves in your stomach even now, doesn't it?"* "Yes it does." *"You want a healthy baby, don't you?"* "Yes I do." *"This baby is not mature yet, it needs a couple of more weeks to grow inside there, doesn't it?"* "Yes it does." *"Your family wants the best for you, don't they?"* "Yes." *"The reason why you were brought in in the first place is to help this baby to mature and prepare for life as well in the best possible way?"* "Yes." *"Has the doctor examined you?"* "Yes he has." *"Is the doctor a trained specialist?"* "Yes." *"Is everything provided here in the labour room? There is a bed you can feel comfortable in, there is medicine which helps your body if needed, and you also have me here who talks to you in a kind way. Is it not true?"* "Yes it is." *"And so, would you be willing to cooperate?"* "Yes" she said weeping. Then she finally settled down and gave in to the unpleasant, although much-needed therapy.	It is worth noting the structure of the **yes-set**: – First, the questions relate to the baby, specifically to the desire first, then to the experience which is certain (moving). – Then the questions relate to the problem (it needs time to grow) and then to the family in connection with those who want the best for her and so quite rightly took her to the hospital. – From here, the questions relate to the doctor who is a well-trained specialist. – Then, they regard the circumstances in the labour room. And so they arrive almost invisibly from the desired baby through the good-willing family and specialist to the present situation. The introduction of the labour room serves again as a context for positive suggestions: comfort, helps the body, and kind company (**indirect suggestion, positivity**). Don't be afraid, nobody hurts you here.

Original story	**Note**
She already knew the cardiotocography (CTG) machine and so putting the sensors on her did not cause any problems. However, when I prepared the infusion by her bed, she again burst into loud crying. At this time, I complimented her on the brave maternal attitude; just how much she is willing to do for this precious new baby.	When the new obstacle comes (infusion), it is enough to just refer to the brave maternal attitude (**motivating**)...
Then using a double-bid, I asked: "*What do you think, in which arm would the infusion be more convenient?*"	...especially if the mother again has a choice (**repetition, double-bind**).
She stretched out her left arm but added: she has never received such a procedure before and she was afraid to pull her arm just when the needle penetrated. She did not and I constantly complimented on her developing braveness.	Despite the woman's negative anticipation, she shows signs of cooperation by warning the specialist of the possible problem.
I sat on the side of her bed and I started to 'reframe' things for her: *"Zsanett, has anyone from your family had such an experience?"* "No, nobody had infusion before and nobody has stayed in a hospital" she said. *"So now you are participating in an adventure that nobody knows apart from you! When you go home, you can proudly tell that you have explored the entire labour room and you could even try the infusion-therapy! You are going to learn a lot of things here and may welcome many of us as personal acquaintances in the future when you next come by!"*	The fact that the midwife has time to sit down serves the woman's need for company on one hand (staying within the specialist's own limits) (**pacing**), and on the other hand, suggests attention and care (**nonverbal suggestion**). The situation is **reframed** as an 'adventure' from which the young mom can benefit. She can imagine herself in the future (**modelling, future orientation**) in such a way that her family looks up to her because of what she will have been through (**motivating**). The suggestion contains embedded messages regarding the birth (explore the labour-room, learn many things, and get to know many people for when she returns). This **implies** the current therapy's success, as well as the birth, which is going to happen in the future.

Original story	Note
In the meantime, the infusion was continuing slowly. The intravenous medication had an effect too and so the contractions stopped. Zsanett finally completely calmed down.	
Another woman was admitted now who was expecting her third baby. She turned out to be Zsanett's neighbour. They both were very happy to meet now. We could hear their happy chatting and laughing all night long.	Faith begins ...
A couple of days later, I saw her on the Pathology Unit for Expectant Mothers. She welcomed me with a wide smile, gave me a hug, and politely asked: "Katika, can I expect you to be at my labour? Your presence would mean a lot!" I could not resist this request. Since that time, she went home. Her baby grew healthily in her womb and we constantly kept in touch by telephone. I hope Zsanett will gain a pleasant birth-experience when the time comes for her baby to be born. I will surely work towards this!	The good rapport built now and the successful situation serve as a good basis for a future collaboration. The young woman belongs to the rare group of people who can say how the specialist's words beneficially affect her (this does not happen in most cases, which is also fine).

Initial situation	Goal
– Strong connection with the family – Uncertain and anxious mother	– Take over emotional connectedness – Motivation for therapy – Calming and relaxing – Positively prepare birth for the future

DESCRIBER OF THE CASE: Zoltánné Gyurkovics, Midwife.

THE FIRST EDITION: Exam paper for the postgraduate training program on Suggestive Communication in Somatic Medicine, co-organised by the Hungarian Association of Hypnosis and Semmelweis University School of Medicine, Budapest.

“Fucking machine”

Original story	Note
A young lady was taken urgently to the operating room with abruptio placentae[3]. She hardly spoke any Hungarian, relying mostly on intonation when spoken to. She was in the terminal stage. The bleeding was noticed just on time and her heartbeat was good. The team takes time to get organised.	
I am trying to reassure her: *“Everybody is preparing to help the baby be born. Everything is all right and the baby will be born in a couple of minutes. Then, my colleagues will examine him and we will take care of it so that you can get some rest. When you wake up after the operation, you will feel stronger than before.”*	The hustle of the specialists is explained (**informing, positivity**). The specialist also explains to her why the operation is necessary (**goal, future orientation**), emphasising that the baby is okay (**positivity**). This also explains why urgent intervention is needed now. She tells her in advance what will happen to her when she is unconscious (**informing, positivity**). This happens with great care, stressing the interest and health of the newborn. How the mother will recover after the operation is also referred to in advance: she will rest and get better (**positivity, future orientation**). This provides a positive frame to the fact that the baby will not be born in the natural way, and therefore, will be separated from his mother after the birth.
My colleague agrees: “There is nothing particularly wrong, but we’d better be quick. We are only waiting for a doctor now.”	Unfortunately, her words imply possible problems (**negative implication**). The phrase ‘we are only waiting for a doctor’ is not really reassuring in this situation…

3 The premature loosening of the placenta.

Original story	Note
The soon to be mom looks at me, frightened: "Is there something wrong?"	The mother understands the negativity. It is worth noting that she asks the one that she is in rapport with, from who she has received reassurances from before.
"No, there isn't. The placenta has started to fall as a result of the contractions. The reason why we are going to the operating room is for the baby to be born sooner. If necessary, we will give him oxygen and liquids. Can you hear just how excitedly the baby's heart beats? The two of you are going to meet soon!"	This is one of those rare cases when denying is correct: there is no problem at all. The mother openly asked if there is a problem or not. However, the answer is short and does not repeat the word 'problem'. The specialist immediately continues to inform the mother in a factual and then positive way. The information lists what is happening as a fact and the prospective reasons about the necessity of the operation (**positivity, informing**). It also informs the mother about opportunities that the doctor has in order to provide for the safety of the baby (oxygen, liquid). The style ('we') also conveys that the specialist stays with the mom and expands the positive rapport to the colleagues she had formed with her previously. The mother's attention is drawn to the 'excited heart beats' which positively reframes the whole situation: the busy atmosphere turns into excitement (**reframing**). 'You are going to meet soon' is the main message (**positivity, future-orientation, motivation**).
She smiles. We help her onto the car and then to the operating board.	Correction was successful.
I think I won another battle. Wait, no I did not. The anaesthesiologist comments over the head of the still-conscious mother: "This fucking machine again…! I can hardly see what is happening on the screen."	No comment…

Initial situation	Goal
– Frightened mother – Unplanned operation – Negative suggestions from colleagues	– To calm the mother – Emphasise the positive outcome – Preventing negative suggestions and environmental effects

DESCRIBER OF THE CASE: Réka Magassy, Midwife Student.

THE FIRST EDITION: Magassy, R. (2010) Csata (Bagatell). /Battle/ *Hipno-Info, 2010 téli száma,* 165. oldal.

Forest

Original story	Note
I met Katalin six years ago when she was expecting her first baby. At that time, I had been working in my new workplace for a year when the possibility of choosing a midwife came into practice in Hungary. She was the first woman who asked me to accompany her in her birth process. It was a curious wish since she knew in advance that she would be having a caesarean (she had hypertension, was overweight, and because her birth status was uncertain, she and her doctor agreed on an elective caesarean). Her doctor told me Katalin wanted to meet me. First I did not understand why Katalin wanted a midwife if she was having a caesarean. Of course the doctor knew her better than that and he added: 'even the person who sticks the tube in her arse to do the enema matters to her'. Later when we met, I started to understand the reasons behind Katalin's decision: she is constantly anxious, was phobic to being pregnant a couple of years prior, and ever since she received treatment and stayed in touch with her psychologist. To be honest, I did not really know how to support her apart from being kind and understanding. For years after the birth, I only heard of her through her doctor. Then, about six months ago, we met again in the hospital. She was a half-term pregnant woman at the time and she and her family excitedly awaited the new baby. Interestingly, it was only a couple of days before the day that I met her when I had been wondering what happened to them after the previous birth. Just like the previous time, we were planning on a 'mutual birth'. This time, however, I could apply what I had just recently learned at the suggestive communication training. At least, this is what I hoped.	The previous connection provides an excellent opportunity to re-establish good **rapport**.

Original story	Note
In the morning of the operation, following the usual preparations (enema, shaving, shower, fitting the infusion, and giving medication as prescribed by the doctor), we were waiting for her husband and the operation. We were in a one-bed room, listening to the baby's heart beat. Katalin was very nervous and I tried not to leave her alone. She was afraid that her heart would 'jump out' or that she would have a panic attack. She was also worried about what would happen in the operating theatre.	The presence of the well-known midwife is indeed a relaxing factor.
As the first step, I told her: *"How wonderful is it, that we are here again and soon you can hold your much awaited baby in your hands! Listen to her calm, rhythmical heart beat; just how peacefully he is waiting to be given birth."* I asked what sort of smells she likes. I brought a scented candle. The light of the candle might also remind her about peaceful relaxation. She left it up to me to choose the music and so I put on a 'foresty' relaxation tape. I will refer again to this later on.	The mention of 'again' reminds her of the previous good **rapport** as well as anticipating the undeniable success of the first birth (**yes-set**). Then comes the **future-oriented** key-suggestion (**goal**): 'you can soon hold your baby in your hands', mixed with a new fact (his heart beat can be heard). This is further accentuated by carefully selected adjectives which turn the situation into a pleasant, rhythmical, and peaceful one (**reframing**).

Original story	Note
Her husband was still not there when I could see the fear taking over. She put this into words: "*I think my heart rate is increasing!*" "*It is a natural phenomenon just before an operation, if someone looks forward to an event. The biological background is the increasing level of adrenaline. This is useful at this time because it affects the baby and helps him adjust to the outside world. This works in the same way and when giving birth happens the other way. We know how well it helps the baby in labour!*" (in the meantime I took her blood pressure and it was completely normal). "*You are both well and can soon see each other and you can touch and stroke you baby.*"	The woman in labour can anticipate the possible coming of sickness. The specialist replies to this immediately by means of **reframing** it as natural 'waiting' for the event. Don't worry, nothing will go wrong! This is accompanied by professional **informing** which leads to benefits. Following the principle of progressivity, first, the 'problem' is turned into a natural reaction and then into a benefit. In the meantime, the previously mentioned word, 'help' returns again and again; but now the mother helps the baby. The situation is closed by a future-oriented target suggestion: the first meeting with the baby is described in different modalities by the specialist (sight, touch).
She was good at controlling herself, although she was still visibly nervous. Since she had mentioned before that she sometimes does relaxation, I told her that this technique may help in the present situation as well. She agreed happily.	Despite the previous steps taken, relaxation did not seem to suffice. The specialist noted this and acted accordingly. It is now an important benefit that the midwife has known the woman for some time and that she is aware of Katalin's experience with relaxation.

Original story	Note
"Kati. Take a position which is the most comfortable for you and for your baby, which relaxes you the most. In this pleasant and relaxed position, you can feel your muscles relax. Your head rests on the pillow and your eyes close. Your breathing lifts your chest very smoothly so that the fresh oxygen can dissolve in your circulation and take the valuable substances to the right place, both in you and in your baby. Good... just like that... nice and slowly... such a pleasant feeling in your body... Imagine yourself in a pleasant and beautiful place where you feel comfortable. This relaxes you... it is so great to be here... you feel infinitely calm and relaxed. Enjoy this beautiful place. And you will be able to think back to this wonderful and pleasant feeling whenever you like. You just close your eyes and think of your favourite place... and this peaceful and relaxed feeling will emerge again. When we are in the operating theatre, you will hear many sounds that you will be unfamiliar with. Such sounds include the sounds of machines, which help the doctors observe your basic functions so that everything can work safely. Therefore, you won't need to bother with these sounds and lights yourself and you can wait calmly for your baby to arrive. You will be able to distance yourself from what is happening in the theatre any time you want by remembering the feelings of this pleasant place. And now, slowly and calmly, you can return here to the labour room where we can wait quietly for your baby to be born."	They start with a series of suggestions which support relaxation (posture, pillow, and breathing), which is followed by the picture of a favourite place. Here, the specialist speaks openly: she does not tell the woman what this pleasant place is; the mother can use her imagination. The positive adjectives appearing in the text are repeated often (comfortable, calm, relaxed, pleasant, beautiful, and wonderful). The scene described by the suggestions is defined with 'here and now' language. This further emphasises the reality of present time (i.e. 'good to be here' instead of 'how nice it would be if you were here'). The specialist makes the current pleasant situation transferrable to the future in a way that is controllable by the woman (**giving a sense of control**). At the end of relaxation, the activities in the theatre are also reframed: the disturbing sounds and lights receive a helping and safe meaning. The ability to distance herself is repeated again (**giving a sense of control**) and is accompanied by positive adjectives: pleasant, relaxed, and restful.

Original story	Note
In the meantime, her husband had arrived and so I left them so they could be together with each other. She felt visibly better and admitted that her relaxation felt really good. In the operating room, following spinal anaesthetics, the usual things happened: lying down, washing, and isolation. Dressed up, I waited for the newborn to arrive.	
A couple of minutes after starting the operation (the doctors were busy with cutting the peritoneum), the spinal anaesthetics worked perfectly. Suddenly, Kati spoke: *"I feel awful, I am going to faint!"* No abnormalities could be seen on the screen: blood pressure and oxygen saturation were all right, her pulse was a little higher than usual but with a good rate. There was no bleeding around the area of operation. Thus, there was no physical cause to the sickness.	The specialist checks for a possible physical cause of the sickness. Objectively speaking, there is nothing wrong which would justify such a sensation.
When I came to my conclusion (about physical causes), I immediately told her about it: *"Kati, everything is all right! Just remember what we discussed! You are able to recall that pleasant place where you have just been!"* *"Yes yes, I know..."*	This helps the midwife genuinely use suggestions which can help the woman relax: in the critical situation, one can use a series of short, 'raw,' and **direct suggestions.** Putting the suggestions into a positive framework, but practically instructing the woman to recall that pleasant place. The wording refers again to the subjective reality: 'where you have just been'. This is not spiced up with anything that may dull the sensation (i.e. what she imagined or what I talked about). The suggestion refers to the direct experience that 'she has been there'.

Original story	Note
The whole intermezzo only lasted for a couple of seconds after which the events continued without interruption. A healthy baby was born who suckled on Kati right after she was taken out of the operation theatre. All three, mother, father, and baby, were very happy.	The intervention is successful.
A couple of days after the birth, we talked about the time Katalin spent in the operating room. She told me that unlike other people who imagine a beach or the sea in a similar situation, she thought of a forest. It was a particular forest where she spent her childhood and had taken her son a couple of times. She is very keen on this forest and was happy that she was able to take her son there too. The soft music helped her to really feel relaxed and restful when she opened her eyes. In the operating theatre when she said she felt unwell, the same sensation came to her which used to signal the start of panic attacks. She got really scared that something bad would happen to her and to her baby but hearing my voice (I stood behind the folding screen, waiting for the baby with a sterile cloth) and remembering what we discussed, she managed to recall the forest and pleasant feelings that came with it. Because I am not a psychologist, I have never felt the power of words with such concreteness before. It was an astonishing experience.	

Initial situation	Goal
– Excitement and unsettlement – The beginning of a panic attack	– Calming down – Prevent the development of a panic attack

DESCRIBER OF THE CASE: Ágnes Rákócziné Krämer, Midwife, Perinatal Advisor, Lactation Specialist (IBCLC).

THE FIRST EDITION: Exam paper for the postgraduate training program on Suggestive Communication in Somatic Medicine, co-organised by the Hungarian Association of Hypnosis and Semmelweis University School of Medicine, Budapest.

Looking for My Money...

Original story	Note
During the night duty on the intensive care unit, I was called on the telephone and informed that Mr. J.K. had become very confused. I went to see him and I found Mr. J.K. in his bed in a coiled-up position (Mr. J.K. had had a gastrotomy because of his peptic ulcer and he was subsequently sent to our unit because of his serious concomitant illnesses. The operation had gone well and the postoperative period had seemed to be smooth until this particular incident). When I entered the hospital ward, I overheard a strange word exchange: "No, nobody wants to steal your money. Please believe me."	The late night call suggests that the people around the patient have already unsuccessfully tried several things to settle the patient down.
I stepped up to the patient: *"Good Evening."* "Go away," was the reply. *"What would you like to do?"*	The arriving doctor is calm and greets the patient according to the basic rules of personal meetings (**building of rapport**). After the rejective answer, the doctor turns towards the patient with an open question: "What would you like to do?" The gesture of giving a **feeling of control** conveys that the patient has (can have) wishes, decisions, and scope of action (In contradiction to the 'typical' negative answer overheard upon arrival: 'No, nobody wants to steal your money. Please believe me').

Original story	Note
"I am going to get my money. I won't let all of my money be stolen!" (I shake hands with him) "*I am Gábor Székely, the doctor on duty. Do you know where you are now?* "Of course," he says, but looks uncertain. "*Well, I'll tell you, after an operation, a lot of people do not know exactly where they are. It's absolutely natural.*"	The doctor can size up the situation based on what he overheard when he came in (namely that the patient is looking for his money). The paranoid way of the operation is also becoming inevitable. Then the doctor introduces himself by shaking hands (**deepening of the rapport, reality orientation**): by mentioning the undeniable facts of the real situation in advance (namely his name and position) he asks the question, "Do you know where you are now?" After the patient's uncertain response: 'of course', he is given information about other people with reality orientation problems in connection with surgery (**informing**). At the same time, the doctor adds that this phenomenon is natural. This way he gives informations about the real situation, allowing the patient to keep control and personal dignity (**indirect communication**).
He interrupts, "Where is my money?" "*I think it was left at the surgical department.*" "All of my things have been stolen!" he shouts angrily. (I call him by his first name) "*J., you must remember you had surgery yesterday at the surgical department of the Kútvölgyi Street Hospital. After the operation, you came here to us, to the intensive care unit at the Kútvölgyi Street Hospital. We'll take care of you for a few days. The surgical department is on the fourth floor and we are on the second. So all of your belongings, your clothes, papers, and money, are at the surgical department in the wardrobe where you left them. Do you need anything now?*"	The patient is still heatedly looking for his money. The doctor factually and calmly answers. Calling the patient by his first name further deepens the **rapport**. After the **direct suggestion** 'you must remember,' he tells the events of the previous period with a lot of facts (**informing**). The information ends with another open question of "do you need anything now?" It strengthens the **feeling of control** just like the previous open question did (**repetition**).

Original story	Note
"I want to go take a bath." *"You know, J., the operation went well and your stomach is healing nicely. Can you feel the bandage protecting your stomach?"* I take his hand and put it on the gauze dressing on his stomach. *"To make sure the operation site heals well, we have to make sure your bandage doesn't get wet."*	The patient changes his attitude: he would like to have a bath. It is a step in the right direction because he has given up on looking for his money and the accusations, but at the same time, it complicates the situation because basically, a negative answer has to be given to this request, too (he cannot go anyway). Instead of an abrupt refusal of the patient's demand, the doctor offers options with a positive fact-string of four components (**yes-set**). You know (**repetition**), J. (**strenthening the rapport**), the operation went well (1), your stomach is healing (2), can you feel the bandage? (3), and protecting your stomach (4)? (I take his hand and put it on the gauze dressing on his stomach). The following period describes close cooperation among the healers and the patient (**rapport**): To have the place of the operation healing well you also have to take care of your bandage. We cannot get it wet. Observe that the doctor never mentions words like 'injury' or unfavourable outcomes such as 'become infected', 'become waterlogged', etc (**positivity**).
"I want to wash myself." *"Certainly, you will have a chance to it and moreover, you will get help too. The nurses will help you get cleaned up within about an hour. They'll give you a hand with everything."*	The patient repeats his desire: the 'going home' gets behind, he focuses only on cleaning up. The situation is easy from here on because this wish can be fulfilled. At the end of this exchange, the doctor calls the patient's attention to the upcoming help of the nurses (**rapport transfer**).
In reality, this conversation lasted only a few minutes. Mr. J.K. cooled down and did not leave for a bath. Neither did he keep on looking for his money any further.	

Initial situation	Goal
– Short-tempered and accusatory patient – Temporarily damaged reality orientation and negative trance state	–Termination of the negative trance – Restoration of the reality orientation – Promoting cooperation with the healers

DESCRIBER OF THE CASE: Gábor Székely Dr., Anesthesiologist-Intensive Therapy, Oxycologist-Emergency Specialist, Psychologist.

THE FIRST EDITION: Exam paper for the postgraduate training program on Suggestive Communication in Somatic Medicine, co-organised by the Hungarian Association of Hypnosis and Semmelweis University School of Medicine, Budapest.

Brain Tumour

Original	Note
A 49-year-old woman arrives to the hospital from hospice home care by ambulance along with her husband. We have treated her previously with symptoms originating from her brain tumour. However, her symptoms have intensified recently as a result of increasing pressure in her brain, which was the very reason she was admitted to the hospital this time (at a previously agreed appointment, with the consent of the patient). The doctor in charge informs me about the arrival of the patient. The reason why he consulted me is because the patient was reluctant to provide answers at the anamnesis and rejected all sorts of help, including the brain-pressure relieving injection. The doctor asked me to 'do something' as he is powerless without the patient's cooperation.	
As I enter the patient's room, the husband stands up and is ready to leave. I ask him to stay.	The psychologist decides to include the husband. The family of the patient is psychologically just as well involved in illness as the patient is, especially if she needs constant care. Therefore, it is important for the husband to witness and perhaps be actively involved with the decisions that we make.

Original	Note
I introduce myself to the patient, then to the husband, and I ask permission to sit down.	The introduction is an 'obligatory' **rapport building** element. In this case, by introducing herself to the husband as well, the psychologist encourages him to stay (**repetition**). The fact that the psychologist takes a seat implies that she is willing to stay as long as needed, to pay attention, and to listen. By asking permission to do this, the patient and her husband are given the freedom of choice and autonomy which was probably unexpected. This small gesture conveys that 'anything that happens here is with their consent; you are actively participating in everything'.
I ask the patient how she feels, where she came from, and why. I learn from her that she was taken from home by the ambulance. She is scared because she does not know what to expect here. "I can barely think because my head hurts so much".	Despite the specialist's previous enquiry about the patient (from the doctor), she asks about her arrival. It is noteworthy that all her questions are open-ended and that she does not mention any negativity (i.e. Are you feeling very bad? You cannot bear it any longer? etc.: **positivity**). The 'why did you come here?' question is especially important since this in itself can remind the patient of the reason she came in (which she obviously wants to achieve: **motivation**). These questions, especially the one regarding her reason, accentuate the message even further (which was started by the permission to sit down): the patient is not a passive object but an active participant of the treatments (**repetition**). The answers to the open-ended questions provide important information (about the uncertainty and fright of the patient).

Original	Note
"I can see you find it hard to speak." "Yes, the doctor came too and asked all sorts of questions. She wanted to give me an infusion, but I don't want anything, I have had enough of medications."	The psychologist's observation obviously finds open doors (**pacing**). The patient's response immediately leads to the key problem (accepting infusion). Luckily, it is the patient herself who brings it up, and at the same time, explains her decision.
"You have taken loads of medication since you have been ill." "And they have no effect. I am sicker and sicker." *"You find it hard to trust drugs. I understand."*	Another undeniable statement from the specialist: **yes-set** is forming. Although the patient's answers are short, she is opening up more and more. The psychologist mirrors her answers (**pacing**), but reframes them a little: Instead of 'has no effect' she says 'it is hard to trust' which implies a better drug effect. The response supposedly finds acceptance with the patient, and at the same time, opens up another opportunity, instead of complete refusal of the medication. The phrase 'I understand' expresses the specialist's empathy which brings the two people closer to each other.
"And the doctor urges me so much. I don't even know if she has read all my papers." *"You can be certain about the doctor's cautious care. She always starts her visits by reading all documents of the newcomers."*	Why is she so mistrustful? Another important set of information emerges: the patient felt as if the doctor rushed too much and therefore she openly expressed her mistrust with this doctor (as well). The specialist's response is a factual and confidence filled declaration regarding her colleague.
"I thought everyone is given the same thing here." *"Not at all. It is very important to provide individually tailored treatment. This can be different in each case and everyone has their best suitable combination. This is why the doctor is here: to learn what you need."*	The patient pronounces that she had misconceptions about the unit. To clarify this, the psychologist provides many facts about the practice of the hospital: in a positive way, often **repeating** the key suggestions: 'the best suitable', 'what you need'.

Original	Note
"But I can't even think anymore, I don't even know what I want or why my head hurts so much. What shall I do now?" *"Would you allow me to make a suggestion?"* "Well, yes, that'd be great because I can't even think anymore."	The patient asks for advice. They got here from complete rejection by a couple of sentences. In spite of this, the psychologist does not immediately give an answer. Instead, she asks for permission (**repetition**) to give advice. This further supports the patient's autonomy. It is important that the advice arrives in response to the patient's explicit demand.
"I suggest you accept the excellent infusion that your doctor recommended. This will soon improve your comfort, put your head right, and will allow you to again be able to think. Then you can discuss everything with the doctor: what you want and what you don't want."	At this point, the psychologist decides to suggest "only" (**repetition**). She lists a series of positive suggestion: (1) infusion is good, (2) it will improve your comfort, and (3) put your head right. This will 'heal' the patient's complaints, notably that she is unable to think. The effect is further strengthened by referring to the time *after* the infusion is received (**future orientation**). This will do you good since you will be able to discuss with the doctor what you want (**motivating**). This is of course another attempt to highlight the patient's autonomy and active involvement in her treatment.
"Well, if you say so… All right then." *"So can I call the doctor and the nurse so that they can bring the infusion?"* "Sure, let them come."	The patient accepts the suggestion; however, she is encouraged to pronounce it again: the infusion may come (**positivity, repetition**).
Following her positive response, I said goodbye and wished her all the best with the infusion ("*You will see that your thinking will become clearer drop by drop*"). I then ran to tell the doctor to hurry up while the patient is facile.	**Positive suggestions** in relation to the infusion are listed again (**repetition, direct suggestions**). There is no doubt what so ever regarding the effectiveness of the infusion – i.e. 'we hope everything goes well, etc.'

Original	Note
As it turned out later, the patient was extremely helped by this small act and she became one of our most 'thankful' patients. A few days of treatment resulted in a significant reduction of her symptoms, after which she was ready to leave the hospital and to be cared for at home.	

Initial situation	Goal
– Resentful patient – Pain	– Acceptance of the suggested treatment – Develop trust with the Unit and the specialists

DESCRIBER OF THE CASE: Eszter Biró, Counselling Psychologist

THE FIRST EDITION: Case report to this volume

Shower

Original story	Note
At this time, I arrived for my night duty at the delivery room. The doctor on duty, my dayshift colleague, and the cleaning lady were sitting in the midwives' room like a "defeated army". At last you came, they said, do something with the mother to be in labour because they have tried everything.	The fact that the colleagues are exhausted and have run out of ideas adds an extra burden to the situation. The "invitation" is public so the result of this intervention will also be public. These circumstances are inspiring for some (while it can put off others).
The expecting woman was standing in the shower (in the shower room) next to the delivery room and was constantly screaming that she could not take it anymore.	The signs of negative trance are evident. Do not waste your energy with screaming because you'll get exhausted this way!
She was young, twenty-one years old and was expecting her first baby. Nowadays such a young mother to be is rare. There were some piercings and tattoos on her body. Her partner was with her in the shower but he was also seemingly in despair. I had the impression that the baby was not planned and that their relationship was not too old.	Based on the first description, the midwife's opinion about the woman and the couple is not very favourable. What is more, at the moment, she does not seem to regard the father as a real partner.
She was fighting with all her strength against the pains, she tried to escape from the situation.	
I introduced myself, then in the next moment, due to a strong contraction, her whole body got tense and I could witness a contraction, accompanied by an eardrum-splitting sound effect.	Regarding the establishing of **rapport**, the introduction is a crucial factor. At first, the midwife is only a passive observer in the situation.

Original story	Note
I praised her for handling it very well. During the next sign of pain, I encouraged her to let out an even stronger and stronger voice. Let the whole delivery room know when her womb is working and when her baby is pushing its way through.	The key to the solution: she does not try to "advise" her against screaming, but accepts it, and, what is more, encourages it (**paradox suggestion**, first element of "**pacing**"). She gives a different meaning to the screaming of the woman in labour – in contrast to what has been going on so far (**reframing**): it is the signal, the message of the natural processes of birth, the job of the womb. To this she connects the expected objective: the coming out of the baby (**positivity, future orientation**).
We were doing this throughout several contractions. I then asked her to notice when her abdomen is soft and when her womb takes a rest so that she can have a rest, too. I asker her to signal this to me by inhaling slowly, very slowly, and by exhaling even more slowly.	Directing the attention toward the rhythmic functioning of the womb takes place. For this, she anticipates the possibility of "rest" (**motivating**), as the mother who is in labour has been like this since the morning and must be extremely exhausted. The midwife asks signals of all this (**strengthening the rapport**) and assigns a task which supports the goals to achieve calmness, lessening agitation, and physiologically (i.e. slow breathing).
At the beginning, rest was not achieved between contractions. She wanted to scream the usual "I can't take it anymore" by all means. I asked her to pay attention to when the pains were coming, as I needed to know, (to) help me. She could only scream during the contraction, but then as loud as possible.	Despite the seeming failure (i.e. that there is no rest achieved), the strategy used so far continues. Screams during contractions (and not pains, **positivity**) are prescribed / allowed (**pacing** element **repeated**), but at the same time, it is restricted as well (**leading**).

Original story	Note
For another quarter of an hour I still had to dictate the "Rest, Scream" rhythm and then the screaming was nicely and gradually replaced by slow exhaling and involuntary pushing. Her body was not tense either. After two hours, she delivered her baby boy without a sound.	With the "dictation" in line with the established rapport, the midwife takes over the leading: the **pacing-leading** elements reach their goal here. The phrasing of "we rest, we scream" in first person plural is already the reflection of the first joint action (**sustaining rapport, compliance**) The professional does not expect immediate results (**the principle of successive approximation**), but rather that the slow breathing, relaxation, and getting attuned to the natural rhythm of birth will slowly emerge.

Initial situation	Goal
– Labouring woman in negative trance – Tries to escape the situation – Her focus is on pain	– Establishing rapport – Introducing relaxing periods into the continuous stretching – Redirecting attention to the bodily signs during delivery

DESCRIBER OF THE CASE: Katalin Kondor, Midwife, Perinatal Advisor.

THE FIRST EDITION: Exam paper for the postgraduate training program on Suggestive Communication in Somatic Medicine, co-organised by the Hungarian Association of Hypnosis and Semmelweis University School of Medicine, Budapest.

Scrubbing

Original story	Note
The patient barely managed to communicate during assisted breathing, following extubation. We learnt from the family that the patient is unable to write or read. He had previously been treated with respiratory diseases, but has never been assisted with breathing. During the treatment, an attempt was made three times to extubate him, but every time he went back on the machine because of exhaustion.	The shadow of unsuccessfulness evidently lies upon the fourth attempt.
"How are you feeling?" "Not well!" *"You look a lot better than yesterday!"* (and I mean this). … (no answer) *"You again breathe on your own! Without help! You are doing it very well."* "But it's hard!" *"The normal, healthy state returns."*	What's the problem? The doctor starts with an open-ended question (How are you feeling?). He does not mention fatigue, disappointment, etc., which would logically come after all that has happened. He starts with positive facts (**yes-set:** you look better, breath on his own, without help). The doctor ascents the important suggestions (you are doing it well, the normal, healthy state returns). The last sentence is formulated without any reference to uncertainty (i.e. we hope, maybe, if everything goes well, etc.) and declares positive outcome (**positivity, future orientation**).

Original story	Note
"They have put this stuff in me many times already!" (he points at the respiratory machine) *"Yes, we took a break three times already. You must remember, you have been without this stuff a little longer each time. Today's examination shows that you have fully recovered from pneumonia. You are fully recovered! Now it will be easier without that stuff. We'll break a record today, shall we? You are breathing so well that you don't need this stuff anymore."*	The doctor immediately **reframes** the patient's sorrowful comment: the (apparent) failure appears as a pause. This is pounced in plural: '*we* have kept a pause' (**rapport, cooperation**). This is immediately followed by the facts (every time a little longer without the machine, promising results of the examination). The just-mentioned positive future-orientation further accentuates the main message: (which has also been prepared by a couple of facts): he has fully recovered. The doctor repeats this with the patient three times (stuff) which he links **pacing** with. All together, the facts lead to positive outcomes (**leading**) (will be easier, break a record, you don't need this stuff). The form 'we' appears again which affirms the **cooperation** between the doctor and the patient.
"I would like to go home." *"Good. When would you like to go home?"* "Now" *"Would you like to know what you need to do to go home as soon as possible?"* "Yes I would."	At first sight, a completely non-relevant need of the patient (he wants to go home) is only clarified as the response to the doctor's question: it is out of the question that he would not go home; only the exact time needs to be clarified. Thus, the patient is offered a reason which may motivate him the most (**motivating**). The doctor replies with a question even to the bit rushing '*now*' response. Would you like to know what you need to do to go home as soon as possible? The yes response is the first sign of cooperation on behalf of the patient.

Original story	**Note**
"I'll tell you. We have a physiotherapist here, whom I will shortly introduce you to. She will help you today. She will tell you how best you can use your lungs now that you have regained your strength in the last couple of days. She will show you how to do breathing exercises so that you can do them on your own. You will nicely cough out the discharge and everything else that needs to come out. All right?" "Yes."	Another six-step **yes-set:** I tell you (1), we have a physiotherapist (2), I will introduce you to (3), she will help you today (4), she will show you (5), and help (6) which leads to the important suggestions: 'to best use your lungs', 'now that you have regained your strength' and 'you can do them on your own'. The cooperation is expanded to the physiotherapist (**rapport transference**) and positive future-orientation appears.
The patient nicely worked with the physiotherapist, but the patient started to give up when she left. He did not cough unless he was told to, although a lot of discharge would come up in this situation.	This is where the effect of the last conversation wears off…
"What do you like doing at home?" "Washing-up." *"Do you do household chores?"* "Yes." *"Do you have any other job?"* "No." *"So do you look after the whole family?"* "Yes." *"They look forward to you going home, don't they?"* "Yes, they do." *"What is your favourite chore?"* "Scrubbing." *"What do you scrub?"* "Dishes." *"You see, here you have to do the same job. What you like. Only that you don't need to do the dishes, but your own respiratory tracts. Do you deal with dishes that are very dirty?"*	The doctor reminds the patient of the previously mentioned main motif of going home (**motivation**). Note the open and direct question (you *like* instead of you *would like*). The doctor links the patient's favourite home job (scrubbing) with what needs to be done now (**metaphor**).

Original story	Note
"Yes I do." *"What do you do with them?"* "I scrub them." *"What do you scrub them with?"* "Hypo." (As this is a strong domestic antiseptic, I was a little surprised here and was distracted: in my head, I was forming a polite rejection to the formal invitation to a dinner). *"And then they are shiny, aren't they?"* "Yes they are." *"So you scrub them until they are nice and shiny."* "Yes." *"Well, scrub your respiratory tracts in the same way now till they shine too! Do you remember what you have learnt from your physiotherapist?"* "Yes I do." *"You have learnt it and now you can do it on your own. As you cough, the discharge will come out and your tracts will became clearer and clearer. You will continue until it is necessary. You scrub the dish until it's not dirty, don't you?"* "Yes, I do." *"Well you just have to cough too until you feel that there is nothing there."* "All right."	Evidently, the patient cleans very dirty dishes so the 'yes' response is not surprising. After the short intermezzo of the hypo, the shiny and clear target emerges in the series of the scrubbing pictures. The numerous affirmations prepare another important suggestion (**yes-set**): You just have to cough when you have to cough, until you feel that there is nothing there.
"That way it is very clean on the inside. So you take a deep breath, then you cough so it clears it out and makes your breathing easier. And when it is completely clear, you can go home and scrub the dishes for the family. They will be very happy to have you back home again."	With the help of picturing the scrubbing, the doctor further strengthens going home (**motivating, metaphor, repetition**). The required activities gain sense in the form of a positive target. In addition, he links it to the happiness of family.
I cannot comment on the fourth attempt of extubation, but six hours after the event the patient is pretty well. He is holding a tissue full of discharge in his hand.	

Initial situation	Goal
– Negative preconceptions following the new attempt of extubation – The patient is under-motivated	– To build a positive future-orientation – To activate and motivate the patient.

DESCRIBER OF THE CASE: Gábor Székely Dr., Anesthesiologist, Intensive-Therapy Specialist, Psychologist.

THE FIRST EDITION: Exam paper for the postgraduate training program on Suggestive Communication in Somatic Medicine, co-organised by the Hungarian Association of Hypnosis and Semmelweis University School of Medicine, Budapest.

Diabetes

Original story	Note
The doctor asked for advice concerning a man. This is what I learned: he suffers from high cholesterol. He has also recently been diagnosed with diabetes (about two weeks ago), so he needs to take insulin. However, he has already been informed about this in another hospital. He arrived with his wife and daughter. They were quite anxious and the little girl was bored.	The situation is 'usual' for the doctor, but trauma for the family. The key to good cooperation is the positive attitude of the whole family.
I began to build the rapport: "*My name is Kriszta Kertész, I am a dietician. You did well coming here to discuss the details of the diet. The reason why the doctor didn't give you any medication for the cholesterol is because you can achieve a lot with the appropriate diet.*"	Informing during **rapport building** is based on facts: they came to see the dietician. This is welcomed by the specialist (**positivity**), and expresses the other, might not be expected, advantage (**positivity** again): the diet helps with cholesterol (**informing**).
Then I started the consultation. I briefly mentioned the blood sugar level as well, which was followed by the wife's surprise: "Really? He can eat this?" Then I began to ask what she was told in the other hospital. It turned out that for two weeks, since the diabetes was diagnosed, his wife was anxious and did nothing but give cries of desperation. She wanted to provide the best possible diet for her husband but they had forbidden everything. And now they are even more desperate because this new problem with cholesterol came on top of it. They feel that they cannot cope and follow all this of this (What happened in the other hospital is that they had received consultation, but only received the conventional information, which they tell an overweight person on pills as well as a normal weight young man on insulin).	It turned out that the family had received 'strange' information in the previous hospital. The shock of diagnosis was topped with the feeling of powerlessness caused by restrictions (and the negative attitudes built on it). Sensitive situation: things have to be sorted out in a way which does not interfere with the principle of collegiality. In these cases, good rapport and honesty are especially important: trust can be built on this so the family is more likely to accept what they hear now than the information they had heard in the other place.

Original story	Note
I started to encourage them and reframe the information and bans they previously received. "*In fact, this is not a diet but a healthy way of eating. Everyone should eat and live like this. This is a healthy lifestyle that we are talking about here. We will develop an individually tailored diet together, taking into consideration sport habits, feasts, and special occasions. He can live a full life; he doesn't need to give up anything.*"	You must not fall into despair; if you keep the diet, hopefully there won't be any problem! Instead of the list of banned things the specialist emphasises that this should be followed by everyone since it is healthy (**reframing**). They develop a solution together that suits the family's lifestyle (**cooperation, rapport**).
I ask them to co-operate; I expect teamwork.	Emphasising cooperation and teamwork pulls the patient (family) out of the negative trance caused by the shock of diagnosis (**dissociation**). This way, the specialist provides emotional and informative support too.
I started with the basics; explaining the causes. I also explained (also by drawings) the role of insulin, its mechanism, and its necessity. The number of times to eat depends on the type of insulin. I draw the effect graph, and so they understood why it is necessary to eat six times a day.	Explaining the *reasons* behind the 'to dos' helps patients stick to them (**informing**).
I provided the family with choices. The important thing is that they have to eat whole grain bread. I listed many types to choose from. I did the same with vegetables which can be eaten with the morning and evening sandwich. Whatever he likes, is currently available, or they have at home is okay. It really does not matter.	Choice provides a sense of control (**double/multiple-bind**). Possibilities guide the family from the 'there are many things you cannot have' situation into a much more comforting 'these are my possibilities, I can choose' situation. Basically, it is about the principle of **positivity**: 'you can eat/do these' instead of 'you cannot eat/do these'.

Original story	Note
I remained in constant touch with all three of them. I included the little girl too. They liked it. I asked her about family habits regarding dinners, which she may know and experience.	During counselling, special attention should be paid to create a good rapport since in this case, the family is not at all just a passive observant of the conversation; the diet affects the lifestyle of the entire family.
The man plays badminton with his daughter. I tasked the little girl with a serious challenge: take dad to the training and make sure he sweats well (in the last two weeks he even gave up sports, he was too scared).	New opportunities came to light, which as they thought before, they had had to give up. Sports are another area where the cooperation of the family is essential (**cooperation, giving a sense of control**).
I could see on his wife that as time went on, she became more and more relaxed. She was not hostile with me any more but she was rather trusting now. She listed a series of questions (I offered in the beginning that they may ask any questions as we go along).	It is of great pleasure when the patient or the family asks questions: it proves that they are actively involved with what they hear and they trust the specialist who provides them with the information. What is important now is to have the patience and time to answer these questions. In this case, both are provided.
I provided an example from everyday life: the advantages of whole grain pasta (durum pasta). "*You surely have experienced this before; only after half an hour of filling up with pasta you were hungry again.*" They nodded. Through this example I explained the effect and speed of absorption of the different carbohydrates. And as a gratis I added: "*this type of pasta doesn't even contain any cholesterol!*" (**reframing**)	The specialist builds on the family's own experience in providing new elements of information (**pacing-leading, informing**).

Original story	**Note**
I started asking his wife about his favourite dishes and what she normally cooks. She had already given up many of these in the past two weeks. However, re-discussing these dishes, I offered a couple of new alternatives which does not result in having to completely give them up.	Another example of the cooperation with the family and providing individually tailored counselling.
I looked into his blood level diary. I complimented him on how nicely he writes it. The result is already visible; he has good blood level results. I talked about the know-how of checking the blood level. They reacted to this with surprise: why have they not been told about this before? They did it differently before, but it seems better this way.	The compliment increases the man's sense of control in an area in which he had not been familiar with before (**positivity**). They have also received practical advice on taking blood levels (**informing**). Critiquing colleagues is an unpleasant situation. One should not start to take it out on others in front of the patient. Usually it is more sensible to ignore this remark, as it happened in this situation.
At the end of the consultation, I asked if they had any further questions. I offered them the opportunity to return for a control (but in a way that suggests they should only come back for routine tests and not because they have a problem). They should feel free to come back if they feel like it.	Offering the opportunity to return should be put sensibly so as not to imply the possibility of problem or failure. The best is when there indeed is a regular control which is attended by everyone. This opportunity also serves as a tool to maintain rapport as well as expand the sense of trust into the future (**future orientation**); the specialist is open to further cooperation. If you have any problems, come back in.
They were utterly thankful. I could indeed see the sense of relief and relaxation.	

Initial situation	Goal
– Recent diagnosis and despair because of banned things – Negative information in the previous hospital	– Build trust and cooperation (with family members as well) – Offer possibilities and choice – Positively reframe the situation

DESCRIBER OF THE CASE: Krisztina Kertész, Dietician.

THE FIRST EDITION: Exam paper for the postgraduate training program on Suggestive Communication in Somatic Medicine, co-organised by the Hungarian Association of Hypnosis and Semmelweis University School of Medicine, Budapest.

After Trying to Commit Suicide ...

Original story	Note[4]
After an attempted suicide, a young woman is taken to somatic care followed by psychiatric examination. I will present a part of a conversation with her after detoxification. She was being alert but still very much in a critical state of mind.	
"*I was informed that you were taken to the Emergency Room yesterday, in an unconscious state. You were in a critical condition and it looks like you may have poisoned yourself*," I start the conversation this way, after introducing myself and defining the situation.	The facts known by the doctor could be informative to the patient (**informing**) and could initiate a **yes-set**. Introduction and definition of the situation are essential for building **rapport.**
"*How are you now?*"	How could you do that? Such irresponsibility! The question 'How are you now?' implies that the patient could be in a better state of mind compared to the mental state leading to the attempted suicide (**implication**). At the same time, the open question shows a real interest, communicating a chance for a substantive and unhurried conversation to the patient.
"Feelin' nothing much..."	The answer is not necessarily a rejection. It could be the expression of the momentarily inexplicable experience.
"*I see that you are sad... fighting back tears. You must feel awful. Don't you?*"	The doctor's answer comments on the visible signs of an emotional state (**pacing-leading**). The negative question (Don't you?) serves as a reconstitution of resistance.

4 Initial remarks of the original author are also used in the text.

Original story	Note
"Yes...I do," she says crying, wiping tears with her hands.	
"*Will you accept a tissue?*"	Offering the tissue strengthens the previously introduced **yes-set**, especially accompanied by the words "Will you accept."
She nods... still sniffling, looking at, and fumbling with the tissue.	
"*You know, the tissue we get here is made of super absorbent material. It absorbs tears a lot more efficiently than commercially available tissue.*"	Saying 'our tissue is better than the commercial one' sends a message that the patient is in a special environment where emotions and tears are appropriate and welcome. With this, the doctor underlines the previously mentioned ("how are you now?") positive possibilities. It is the object-bound, **indirect suggestive effect** that also turns the patient's inward attention to the outside world.
"Thank you..." Less crying, wiping tears...	
...I am waiting patiently, silently observing the patient's emotions, behaviour, and varying intensity of crying ... looking for an appropriate moment when I could start talking.	The doctor adjusts himself to the patient (**rhythm and pauses**).
"*I would like you to tell me what happened to you*" I ask. "Nothing," she replies.	Patient rejects the doctor's possibly too early attempt to lead. Note the neutral nature of the explorative question: There is no mention of trouble, tragedy, "wanting to die," etc.
"*Maybe you're not able to...or you don't feel like talking about it...*" "Nope."	The doctor takes a step back with a sophisticated indirect suggestion (**pacing-leading**).
"*It can't be easy for you... maybe you are not even sure if you want help... If you would rather rest, we can get back to this tomorrow.*"	The **double-bind** offers a pseudo-alternative, implying that they will definitely talk her story over.

Original story	**Note**
"If you can put up with me and you don't mind me crying… I'd rather talk now." "*All right, look*," pointing at the shelf on the wall, "*there is enough tissue here, and I am listening.*" "I see," she says, still sniffling, but with a shy, thank-you-like smile.	The patient is now ready for conversation. The previous fiasco (a step back because of a too early inquiry) could be an advantage: the patient experiences that the doctor adjusts himself to her rhythm to be ready for conversation. The doctor can mention the tissue as a 'mutual friend' to openly express that he pays attention to the patient.
…(listening, waiting, and communicating an active attention toward her) "I wanted to die," she says with a determined expression. There is a certain childlike defiance in her tone, like saying "now… how about that?"	In a situation like this, it is hard to maintain the silence needed for the patient to open up further: lots of people are tempted to fill the silence with talking.
"*I understand*," I answer. "*The colleagues who pumped all those pills out of your stomach were right. It was an attempted suicide…they saved you…*"	
"I was unable to die", she says. "*You are alive.*" I answer.	Redefining what happened has a key importance. Replacing 'unable to die' with 'staying alive' (**reframing**) and foreshadowing shaping (**future orientation, positivity**).
"Yes," she says, deep in her thoughts. – "I still can't see anything ahead." Her gaze is fixed, staring at seemingly nothing, and she has stopped crying. She looks rather worried.	Patient shows signs of spontaneous trance.
"*To me it seems like you are worried about the future, like about "what's next"… am I right?*" …a small nod, her face is somber, and she does not lift her gaze	The doctor keeps on stressing the **future orientation**, but the patient still shows signs of spontaneous trance.

"*Do you want me to bring you more fancy absorbent paper?*" I raise my voice. (By raising my voice, and using an unusual expression, I'm trying to divert her attention and snap her out from a fantasy I have no way of controlling.)	In the given situation, the professional goal is to snap the patient out of the trance: the doctor tries to direct her attention to the outside world. Even in a tense situation, it is appropriate to use humour.
"Thank you, doctor. See, I'm not crying anymore," she says, seeking eye contact.	The maneuver has been a success. The usage of words and the seeking of eye contact imply an active, here-and-now **rapport.**
"*Yesterday you decided,*" I say, trying to bring her back to our conversation, "*you wanted to die… and now you have these stirring, mixed, and uncertain feelings. You are alive…*"	The phrasing strengthens the patient's **feeling of control.** The indicators of emotions are very carefully selected. Instead of 'fatal, horrible, and hopeless,' he typifies the patient's feelings as sentiments capable of modulation, change, and even of turning into something positive.
"*It will be easier if we look at and talk about what happened… maybe I can help you deal with it. It will be good to clear things up.*"	The **direct suggestions** of 'it will be easier' and 'I can help' motivate the patient for further efforts by direct suggestions, in both kinesthetic (deal with it) and visual (clear things up) modalities.
"*I would like you to tell me what happened to you. Why did you want to die?*"	Previous question **repeated.**

Initial situation	**Goal**
– Resistant patient with impaired alertness	– Building cooperation and motivating coping – Building a future-oriented perspective

DESCRIBER OF THE CASE: Zoltán Ambrus Kovács, Psychiatrist.

THE FIRST EDITION: VARGA K. (ed.) (2011) Beyond the words. Communication and suggestion in medical practice. Nova Science Publisher, New York.

Charlatans

Original story	Note
7 AM, shift change: Approaching the delivery room, an inarticulate scream caught my attention. I was told by the night shift that it had been like this for hours. They had not been able to persuade the mother into using her energies more efficiently. They told me that she was near the end of her dilation phase, but her hips were narrow and they were expecting a big baby.	The night's previous events outline the mother's exhaustion and an overall failure.
I entered the separated delivery room. I saw Ágnes (expecting her firstborn) frantically thrashing about in bed. József (her husband), like a caged lion, was circling around in the room, driven by rage and despair.	The first direct impressions show the signs of very obvious negative trance, not only on the mother but the father as well.
Between contractions, I introduced myself to both of them. Whatever I asked Ágnes, she didn't answer, she even turned her head the other way. When I touched her hand, she abruptly pulled it away and then she shrank back resigned. József could have killed with his eyes. "Why aren't you operating on her? What are you, charlatans or what?" he grumbled. They both radiated distrust, despise, and despair.	In spite of the obvious tension and much negative charge, the professional starts by introducing herself (**rapport**).

Original story	Note
I made an attempt to calm them down, assuring them that everything was going just fine: the baby's heartbeat was good and the mother's body was giving way to the new life bound for the outside world. I asked them to trust the natural functioning of the body and assured them that the end of the all night's ordeal when they could hold their beautiful baby in their arms was very close. I told them that everybody surely would feel the same way under the circumstances. I was encouraging them that their patience and determination would surely lead to success. Unfortunately, I wasn't able to cheer either of them up. They felt that I was saying these words only out of routine, and therefore, nothing would change in their predicament and I would leave them alone in their desperate situation.	The expert's attempts to calm her down and ease the negative tension (**positivity, future orientation, motivating**) do not lead to success (for the time being).
They totally distrusted me, and in their exhaustion they only saw me as an enemy. Then I changed my tactic.	The expert senses that the situation is not under control yet. She modifies her approach.
I sat down in the chair near the bed and watched silently. I was observing the contractions and how the baby's heartbeat reacted to them. I was also watching how the mother's body was functioning. Long minutes passed by.	She turns to the technique of patience and (seemingly) idleness, despite the husband's remark to urge an intervention.
József has stopped pacing and he sat down. Meanwhile, the screaming rhythmically alternated with resignation.	The expert serves as a **model** for the father: he also sat down.
During one of the pauses, Ágnes suddenly turned to me and quietly said: "Thank you for staying."	The new approach has been successful: the woman calmly initiates communication and even expresses her gratitude. A **rapport** is emerging…

Original story	**Note**
"*I know you are suffering and I am here to make your labour easier,*" I said.	The expert's reactions are: wording the woman's feelings (**pacing-leading**) and determining her own role and the mutual **goal** (**rapport**).
"Do you think we can do this?" asked Ágnes. "*Of course, just watch out for the feeling of strength to come,*" I answered.	The woman becomes open to the expert's opinion, though only with a hesitant question at first. However, the answer (naturally) is confident and clear, drawing up the key to the solution: "just watch out for..." She gives the "feeling of strength" as the object of attention, which is a positive and helpful rephrasing of what the woman may have experienced as an excruciating misery (**reframing**). Do you have pain? These weak contractions will do nothing!
Then, a mutually attentive and creative working relationship has started between us.	**Cooperation** and sufficient **rapport** developed.
"*Which position would be the most comfortable right now, sitting on the ball or standing next to the bed?*" I was encouraging her to change her position for her comfort.	Only one question can have many suggestive elements: "*Which position would be the most comfortable* (**positivity**) *right now?*" (**implication:** later on other positions could also be considered) *"sitting on the ball, or standing next to the bed?"* (**double-bind**). Instead of the passive vulnerability, it offers the **feeling of control.**

Original story	Note
I drew her attention to the beneficial usage of the pauses: *"Get some fresh oxygen in your body with a couple of deep inward breaths, then let your muscles relax. Meanwhile, you will feel your limbs become heavy and your whole body will be flushed by a pleasant warmth. Let yourself be absorbed by this pleasant feeling. You can even take a nap. You will experience a rush of energy afterwards,"* I said. *"The stronger the contractions, the better it will feel to relax in between them,"* I drew her attention to the positive effects of rhythmicity.	In this phase, it is appropriate to say such beautiful **positive** suggestions to a previously exhausted, screaming woman. Note the confident and factual words of the expert (**direct suggestions**). There is no doubt of a positive outcome. The "strength" she mentioned in the first reframing comes up again (**repetition**).
From that time on, muscles relaxed, paying attention to the signs of her body, she was consciously focusing her energy on the next challenge instead of lying in bed apathetically and resignedly. During the subsequent raging, stronger and stronger contractions came on and the frantic screams gave way to deep, pristine moans, while I was generously praising her for her efforts: "*Very good, you are doing very well!* " I said.	The change in the mother's behaviour shows the effectiveness of suggestions. The repeated, open, and positive reassurances are especially important.
This went on for more than an hour, while Ágnes was getting better and better at relaxing and using the strength of her muscles by paying attention to the signs of her body. There wasn't a trace of the earlier, endless desperation, accusations, and helpless anger. It was all coordinated hard work. And their child slowly and gradually passed through his shortest but most dangerous passage of a lifetime. At 8.20 AM, Ágnes gave birth to a healthy, 4.80 kilogram, huge baby boy.	

Original story	Note
The woman who previously seemed exhausted, and who had done an enormous job, was now calling her friends and families, crying but jubilant: "I've done it! We have succeeded!" she was shouting into the phone.	

Initial situation	Goal
– Negative trance built on rage and exhaustion – Physical exhaustion and mental helplessness – Father also in negative trance	– Building rapport and cooperation – Turning the negative trance into positive trance – Building trust in the natural functioning of the birth and her own body

DESCRIBER OF THE CASE: Zoltánné Gyurkovics, Midwife.

THE FIRST EDITION: Exam paper for the postgraduate training program on Suggestive Communication in Somatic Medicine, co-organised by the Hungarian Association of Hypnosis and Semmelweis University School of Medicine, Budapest.

The Tooth Fairy

Original story	Note
A six-year-old arrives at the dentist's office with his mother. He has had a toothache for days. His cheek is inflamed. The boy is tired and crabby.	
I sit next to them in the waiting room and I introduce myself to him and to his mom.	Next patient! The doctor goes to the waiting room instead of expecting the next patient to come to his domain (a non-verbal form of **pacing**). This gesture expresses adaptation, attention, and patience ('I have time') towards the patient. It may seem as a waste of time at first, but this will indeed be a good investment in the future if cooperation goes well. He does not neglect the child either. This supports the child's autonomy (**giving a sense of control**), as well as starts building rapport that has to be taken over from the mother in this case.
"You probably know that doctors work in order to help you and the other children," I say.	The declaration of this fact refers to the boy's knowledge and launches a **yes-set,** as well as it strengthens the just-mentioned **sense of control**. The mention of 'help' anticipates collaboration (**reframing**).
"It often happens that children with similar symptoms tell the fish how brave they were in the dentist's chair just before they go home" (There is a fish tank with a couple of colourful fish in it in the waiting room).	New elements of the previously started series (**yes-set**) precede the main suggestion: the child will be brave and go home (**future orientation**). By this, the doctor directs attention immediately to the period following the treatment. She focuses on what is most likely: the child is frightened and wants to go home (**motivating**). She does this in a way that she implies successful treatment as a step toward the much-desired going home. By mentioning 'other children' who behaved so bravely, the doctor sets an example to the still frightened boy (**modeling**).

Original story	Note
"Maybe you will want to talk to them too, won't you?"	The question put in a suggestive (**indirect suggestion**) lead to a strong (internal) answer in the child: 'of course'.
He smiles and bravely enters the dentist's office, tells his problem without my asking, and points to where it hurts. I show him the dental mirror. He takes it into his hand and examines it. Together we have a look at his teeth.	The introduction of the tools, explanation of the steps of the treatment, and examination in cooperation further support the child's **sense of control**.
"Have you noticed how this little tooth wiggles? Maybe the tooth fairy is waiting for it under your pillow already. Look, this pretty little corner is the first sign of your new tooth that would like to come out. Let's help this new tooth to pop up, should we?" He is checking his teeth in the mirror with bright eyes with a wide-open mouth.	The two friendly questions refer to the unavoidable fact that it needs to be pulled out which is further justified by the new tooth trying to come out (**future orientation, informing**). 'Let's help him!' The doctor invites the boy to **cooperate in the decision-making** which finds acceptance as previously prepared by the suggested **sense of control**.
"You just keep your mouth open, we push your milk-tooth out of the way, like a snowdrop sticks its head out from underneath the snow at the end of winter and pushes its hat away. Look, it's out already! We are going to wrap it up so that you can put it under your pillow for the fairy. You have done very well!"	The doctor expresses the expected behaviour (**positivity**). The act itself is **reframed** as 'push away' and something to do together. This is accompanied by a sweet metaphor and the magic image of the fairy mentioned previously. Explicit complementing of the child is not forgotten either.
Of course, he examines his tooth again in the mirror and notes the result with contentment. When I accompany them to the waiting room, he tells the fish happily that his nice and new tooth has come out like a snowdrop.	The previously built-in suggestion gains validity now. This positive experience obviously remains a good basis for future treatments at the dentist's office.

Initial situation	Goal
– Tired and crabby child – His tooth hurts	– Build collaboration – Prevent/dismiss possible fear – Pain reduction

DESCRIBER OF THE CASE: Krisztina Varga Dr., Dentist.

THE FIRST EDITION: Exam paper for the postgraduate training program on Suggestive Communication in Somatic Medicine, co-organised by the Hungarian Association of Hypnosis and Semmelweis University School of Medicine, Budapest.

Pressure Bandage

Original story	Note
A woman with a complex bone fracture is admitted to the Intensive Care Unit following the operation. In the morning of the day after the operation, her wound started to bleed severely. The orthopaedic surgeon recommended a pressure bandage, which had just been started when I got to the Unit. The woman screamed in pain. I had already learned during the handover that the anaesthesiologist has used spinal anaesthetic and nerve blockade. The operation itself lasted for three and a half hours and the patient received three units of blood. The time directly after the operation went all right, the anaesthetics appeared to work, no bleeding occurred, and the patient complained of no pain before feeling the pressure of the wound. When I stepped to her bed, she was short of breath, her eyes were closed, and she occasionally screamed of pain.	
"Good morning, I am Doctor Székely. I can see that your wound hurts a lot." "Yes it does."	The doctor starts with presenting himself and welcoming the patient according to the time of day (establishing **rapport**). These are important elements of the rapport, especially because it includes 'good morning,' which can convey to the patient that her problem is not as severe as not to follow the usual protocol.

Original story	Note
"I am an anaesthesiologist working in this hospital. Like the one who made your operation pain free yesterday. I came to help." She looked up but did not say a word.	The specialist 'takes over the **rapport**' from his previous colleague. He defines himself as a 'helper' (**positivity**). It is important to take over where success occurred – the pain-free operation yesterday. Along with the previous conversation, a **yes-set** is forming: I am Dr Székely (1), I can see your wound hurts a lot (2), I am an anaesthesiologist working in this hospital (3), and like the one who made your operation pain-free yesterday (4), which prepares the target-suggestion: I came to help. The patient manages to establish eye contact in the interaction.
"Everything was all right yesterday, wasn't it? You didn't feel any discomfort during the operation, did you?" "No, it was all right yesterday."	The specialist pronounces: 'it was all right yesterday'. He expects (and receives!) a confirmatory response from the patient. Within seconds, we arrive from 'hurts a lot' to 'it was all right'.
"We can help you today as well to make you as comfortable as possible. And you can help with this too." "How?"	By simply linking yesterday with today, the doctor makes another offer to help (**repetition**). He summons the goal without mentioning pain this time (**positivity**): as comfortable as possible. This **motivates** the patient with talk of success.
"Look at me and hold my hand. I will help you slow down the breathing. You will feel lighter! Take a deep breath (I lift up her hand a little), *then exhale slowly"* (I put down her hand). I am not trying to achieve a normal breathing rate, as we started from 40–50 breaths per minute this time.	Don't be out of breath, this will make it worse! The doctor gives simple and direct instructions to the patient, who is now open to collaboration. They deepen eye contact and touch, which results in deepened **rapport**. The intention to help gets **repeated** too. To the **easy-to-control** exercises (look at me, hold my hand), the doctor links a **direct suggestion** (you will feel lighter), which is followed by new suggestions concerning the breathing. Breathing slower indeed helps with pain management. The doctor conducts the patient with the movement of his hand as well.

Original story	Note
"*Now together!*" (I breathe with her, holding her hand: I lift it up then down, slowly decreasing the rhythm). "*Can you see how easy it is? You might not have thought of just how simply this can be!*"	The two people's synchronicity is expressed on both a physiological and an explicit behavioural level (**pacing-leading**). This is pronounced by the doctor too. The specialist 'announces' the success, calling it 'simple'.
We did really well when she cried up again: "Oh this hurts!" "*You surely sense the pressure on your thigh. This helps stop the bleeding, which is vital. It is very important because you will recover faster. Bleeding stops. Stops. As you breathe slower and slower, you will feel the pressure become duller and duller… And the bleeding stops.*"	The new pain reaction is accompanied by explanations and suggestions: He starts with the obvious (of course she can feel it, she has just said it hurts), however, the doctor does not call it pain, he calls it pressure (**reframing**). He names the reason (**goal**) for it too: to stop the bleeding. This is again followed by what helps and, as a new element, the importance of the aim is also mentioned. The reason for this serves as **motivation** for the patient: fast recovery. The direct aim (stop the bleeding) is expressed many times as a **direct suggestion** (**repetition**). It is only after this that the doctor links the previously successful pain relief suggestion, which leads to decreased breathing. He does this with positive wording (dull), which he repeats. It is a key element in the pain relief suggestions to prepare them; notably to make the patient susceptible by explaining the situation in a positive way and naming the desired aim.

Original story	Note
She slows down her breathing. I dare not to lift her hand because she clings onto it too tightly and I could only force it to move. "*You see just how bravely you are doing it! Well done! It may occasionally happen that you feel the pressure a little more; but it is only temporary. However, this is exactly what you need nowthis helps stop the bleeding. You don't need to do anything else if this happens; you just keep concentrating on your breathing. Breathe in slowly and then breathe out. In and out. This can help you relax too. You only have to breathe and you will relax. You see, you don't even cling onto my hand any more* (she indeed does not). *Can you see how well it goes?*" Eventually she looks at me and smiles a little.	In the new quiet period, the previous suggestions are repeated (you are doing it well). In addition, the doctor 'treats' in advance the possible painful episode in the future. The elements are the same as before: • He calls it pressure (instead of pain). • He says it is only *temporary*. • He justifies it with a positive, recovery-focused suggestion (*this is exactly what is needed*). • He immediately offers a solution (*concentrate on breathing, relax*). The success is again pronounced by the doctor (it goes well), which is reinforced by the patient's eye contact and smile.
From here, she managed to bear the bandage. I could see that she was concentrating on her breathing, but the pain was visible on her. The bleeding practically stopped and she did not need any further transfusion.	

Initial situation	Goal
– Acute pain – Tension and shortness of breath – Strong bleeding	– To normalise breathing and muscle tone – Pain relief – To bear the strong bandage – Stop bleeding

DESCRIBER OF THE CASE: Gábor Székely Dr., Anesthesiologist, Intensive-Therapy Specialist, Psychologist.

THE FIRST EDITION: Case report to this volume.

The Rose

Original story	Note
The telephone rings in the waiting room in anesthesiology: "Zsolt, come to the outpatient clinic. We are going to open an abscess of a teenager and we need venous narcosis," I am told. I go to the outpatient clinic and prepare the anesthesia machine along with the appropriate medication. Meanwhile, everybody arrives (the surgical nurse, the orderly, and the surgeon). We are waiting for the patient. The door opens and they enter. She is holding onto her mother's hand tightly, pressing herself close. In her file, I see that her name is Vali and that she is 13 years old. She has never been under anesthesia. She is noticeably very nervous and she struggles to hold back her tears. She is very anxious; her breath is stressed as she is trying to cover up her state of mind.	The signs of the negative trance, dominated by anxiety, are obviously further affected by the strong bond to the mother.
"Hello Vali. I am Zsolt. We are here with doctor Erika to make sure that during the procedure you can have a nice rest or even a sound sleep if you like."	Establishment of the **rapport** starts as usual: introduction, exposition of the roles, and defining the aim.
She does not even look at me. She keeps staring at her mother.	But it was not enough to break the rapport with the mother and to take over the rapport.

Original story	Note
"I believe you may be a little bit nervous still, but when you are over it and you think back, you will realise it went much easier than you would have ever thought. We will discuss everything beforehand. Nothing unexpected will happen to you. We'll do everything in the best possible way for you."	The expressions of the expert reflect the patient's feelings (**pacing**). Also, in a way, they **imply** the change: 'may be' … 'still'. It is directly followed by a change of perspective from the present situation to the future (**future orientation**), directing the patient away from the momentarily uncomfortable situation (**dissociation**).
"Please, lie down on this table and make yourself comfortable. Easy does it…" Although she lies down on the table, she is still locked onto her mother's eyes. Her mother is looking back and forth to her daughter and to me and is looking a bit confused, asking for help.	There are positive suggestions (**positivity**) in the instructions about the position: the assistant encourages the patient to 'make herself comfortable', giving her a feeling of being in control (**giving a sense of control**). Although hesitantly, the patient follows the instructions. She is still strongly bonded to her mother, thus some more work should be done on the rapport.
"Vali, you can help yourself and us if you slowly sigh a deep sigh and then exhale very slowly. It may be like when the blustering, stormy sea calms down slowly, and everything becomes peaceful."	The new instruction composes the **cooperation** now (to yourself and to us) along with a **metaphor**.
However, there is not much change, so I'll try something else. *"Vali, do you like flowers?" I ask.* She suddenly looks at me. This is her first eye contact with me. "Yes," she says.	The expert realises that the situation is not under control yet. He changes strategy. This brings forth the first positive signs: eye contact, 'yes' answer.
"Girls usually like flowers. Do you have a favorite one?" "I like roses the most…" *"How about a pretend walk thought a rose garden during this procedure?"* I suggest.	He manages to get the patient to interact with the topic of flowers. She now listens to the expert and she readily answers the questions.

Original story	Note
"Will I be pricked? Will it hurt?" she asks.	Yes, unfortunately I must pick you, but don't worry, it doesn't hurt too much! The unexpected questions can be interpreted either about the present situation or the offered rose garden.
"I'll put an infusion line in your arm. This is a really good thing because through this line, I can give you medicine that will help you feel nothing and sleep well."	Before answering the actual question 'Will it hurt?' The expert explains the essence, the **goal**, and the advantages of the procedure (**motivating**) about to be done.
"You will feel it… I can compare it to the prick of a really small and mild rose thorn. It will be over by the time you feel it."	To make the possible feeling concrete, the expert turns back to the rose garden **metaphor** and calls the attention again to the times following the procedure (**future orientation**). He does this all by avoiding words like 'stick a needle in…', 'pain', etc (**positivity**).
"Can we start?" She gives a nod of consent.	He asks for the approval of the patient to start the procedure (**giving a sense of control**). She gives her consent.
"Take a deep breath and exhale slowly." She complies. Meanwhile, I insert the vein cannula. She flinches a little but stays calm.	The patient follows the instruction on breathing.
"See? All done. That was all. Can we go to the rose garden now?" She does not say anything but she closes her eyes.	The comments 'See? All done. That was all.' emphasises that 'only those things happen in here that we have agreed on, just as I promised'. The expert asks for permission again (**repetition, giving a sense of control**) to start the pretend rose garden visit (**metaphor**), giving the patient a feeling of control yet again and he offers his company for the 'walk' (**rapport, cooperation**).

Original story	Note
As I inject the narcotic analgesics, I say, *"We are at the entrance of the rose garden. When you step in, you see two beautiful white roses on your right side."* (She does not say anything and I slowly inject the intravenous anesthetics too.) *"If you step further in, there are three red rose bushes on the left side. You may smell their nice fragrance… Very beautiful, isn't it?"*	The steps of the procedure are followed by unfolding the **metaphor** with the **direct suggestions.**
Erika, the doctor says, the patient is asleep. The procedure starts.	
I make a mental note, surprisingly, everybody was quiet during our communication; this is not typical in this environment. Maybe they were interested in the outcome, I wonder. Sentences of negative suggestion like i.e. 'Don't worry, it won't hurt', 'We'll get this needle into you' 'Stay calm,' etc. were not made.	The positive communication also has its effect on the environment: one of the main advantages is that the patient is relieved of the typical negative messages. Moreover, the beautiful metaphor has a calming effect on the attendants at the same time.
The whole procedure took about six to eight minutes. When we were done, we woke her up. *"Vali, good morning!"* Meanwhile, I stepped up to her and caressed her face with both hands. *"You can take your time waking up slowly if you feel like it."*	Her waking up is greeted with positive words and gentle touches. The rhythm of the wakening process depends on the patient, **giving her a feeling of control.**
"How was the rose garden?" She does not answer, but she starts to stir a little. Suddenly, a wide SMILE appears on her face.	I ask her about the **metaphor** with a big smile. The first experience of anesthesia can be a determining factor for life.

Original story	Note
Erika, the doctor, goes with, and she wakes up completely next to her mother.	The **rapport transference** is put into practice.

Initial situation	Goal
– Anxious patient – Strong bond to the mother	– Release of fear and anxiety – Development of rapport and cooperation

DESCRIBER OF THE CASE: Zsolt Benedek, Anesthesiological Assistant.

THE FIRST EDITION: Exam paper for the postgraduate training program on Suggestive Communication in Somatic Medicine, co-organised by the Hungarian Association of Hypnosis and Semmelweis University School of Medicine, Budapest.

Stuck

Original story	Note
A young woman rolled into a ditch with her car. In the accident, she bruised her chest and supposedly some of her ribs also got broken, causing her intense pain when breathing. Fortunately though, she did not suffer any more serious injuries than these. Nevertheless, she could not get out of the severely damaged car by herself. The technical rescue team was also called in for her rescue operation. I arrived on the spot in an ambulance. By this time, more than a 100 onlookers, the police, and the fire service had already gathered at the scene of the accident as well. When we arrived, two firemen were kneeling beside the wreck, imprisoning the patient. The young woman kept screaming for help. Her face was distorted with terror and she kept saying that she could not breathe and would suffocate in no time.	The injured shows the evident signs of stress and disorientation. The attending specialists, it seems, hadn't been able to calm her down. The situation needs to be resolved in front of a huge audience.
When we reached the car, I first made a personal contact with the patient. "*My name is Csaba Diószeghy. I am an ambulance doctor and I will help you get out of here. I will get you to the hospital as comfortably and as fast as possible. They are already waiting for you there, and soon you will feel much better.*"	This will not be easy. We hardly reach you! Creating contact was exemplary: the introduction, with the full name is the basic element of **building rapport**. The wording conveys professionalism: from now on an ambulance doctor (as well) tends to the patient. All this can also be interpreted as a **yes-set** preparing the following suggestions: the doctor informs the patient about the immediate goal (getting to the hospital); all this is done with the words "comfortably" and "fast" (**positivity**). This information concerning the **future** is followed by a clear, **direct suggestion** (you'll feel much better)

Original story	Note
However, in this case, the patient kept complaining about chest pains and shortness of breath. After a quick checkup, it seemed obvious that her sufficient physiological functions made it possible for the rescue operation to begin. Notwithstanding her complaints, her breathing provided proper oxygenation and her circulation was compensated. However, her lack of cooperation made the rescue operation difficult. A possible pneumothorax (PTX; traumatic PTX) as an underlying cause of her sensation of suffocating could not be safely excluded due to the limited options for examination of the victim. Because of the cramped space, securing the respiratory tracts and ventilation would have been hard to manage, and providing local anesthesia and major analgetic-tranquilisation with the respiratory depressant side effects had increased risks. I tried to delay giving these until we got better access to the patient.	The situation limits the options for the specialist.
So, turning to the woman complaining about chest pains and shortness of breath, I asked the following: *"Where does your chest hurt the worst?"* At the same time, I placed my hand onto her chest. By this time, she was focusing on my hand and indicated that "Yes, it hurts right there".	Asking about the pain is adjusted to what the patient so vehemently tries to convey (**pacing**), and at the same time, also justifies the physical contact (hand placed on the chest), on which the next steps are based. The tender touch is also a way to deepen the contact; the whole maneuver prepares the **compliance** by directing the patient's attention ("At last there is someone who cares about me, and who understands that I am in pain" – can be the experience of the woman). The injured lady's reply now is the adequate reaction to the question of the person involved in the rapport.

Original story	Note
"Alright, now I'll help you get much better, and your breathing will be more comfortable." "O.K.," she replied.	Such an offer would be hard to resist. Let's observe how the wording avoids the expressions 'pain' or 'suffocating'. Instead, it stresses the favorable outcome (**positivity, future orientation**) with sufficient clarity, as already done during the introduction (**repetition**). It is also important to note that all this is not simply stated by the doctor, but he asks the approval of the patient (Alright?). With this action, the **rapport** is strengthened and the patient is provided with the **feeling of being in control.** The negative trance has turned into a positive rapport situation and cooperation.

Original story	Note
"All I'm asking you is to watch my hand and also relax your muscles. When muscles are tense like yours now, they unnecessarily increase pain. So the most helpful thing we can do now is for you to relax your muscles. The easiest way to do this is to become more and more relaxed with each exhalation."	The attention is directed at the doctor: It is easy to get focused onto his hand. However, the relaxation of the muscles is the exact opposite of what has been happening so far: the pain and the fear leads to tense muscles. Therefore, the explanation (**informing**) is important: tense muscles increase pain. At the same time, this wording also permits that pain can have an "adequate" level and only the pain greater than this is considered unnecessary (**implication**). From this statement, the suggestion that pain acts as a signal can be established (**reframing**). The wording now bravely relies on the **compliance:** WE CAN help, and altogether conveys the message that the situation is under control; the doctor knows what to do (**giving a sense of control**). What is more, "the most helpful thing" implies that there are other *possibilities* (**implication**) that further enhance the sense of control, and at the same time, it prepares the switch to a new approach in case this one would not possibly be successful.
While saying the sentence to call the patient's attention to exhaling, I put some pressure on her chest (the painful chest!) with my hand, practically helping her to exhale. Subsequently, I said the sentences synchronised to her exhaling.	The touch and the slight pressure and the sentences synchronised with the breathing demands serious synchronisation, which is led by the doctor at this stage (he adapts, **pacing**).

Original story	Note
"You are getting more and more relaxed, and perhaps you've already noticed how much easier your breathing is becoming this way. With every exhalation, you're feeling better and better." Though I was putting slight pressure on the aching chest, the positive effect of the suggestions was obvious.	The consciously constructed synchronisation with the patient (soft pressure on the chest to the rhythm of her breathing, and saying the suggestions in accordance with the patient's exhaling) enables the doctor to switch to the key suggestions (**leading**): when we can introduce subjects that would have been rejected by the patient at the beginning (easier breathing, physical comfort, sleep-like state, and so on).
Her breathing slowed down. It got deeper and easier as she was following me attentively and she was not complaining about pain throughout the whole rescue. Before the rescue, still in the same situation, I told her: *"Now that you are so nicely relaxed, you will become a bit sleepy, and perhaps you might even fall asleep. When you wake up, you will be in the ambulance and you will also feel how much easier your breathing has become."*	The injured demonstrates the evident signs of following the suggestions word by word. The doctor connects the sleep-like state to the already established relaxation (now that so nicely…), phrasing its occurrence sufficiently "bluntly" ("a bit… perhaps…," **indirect suggestion**). The suggestions depict beforehand what will happen **in the future.** Let's pay attention to the clarity and the confidence of the wording (for example not "if you wake up", but "when you wake up"). In the case of a patient who follows the suggestions in such a direct way (literalism), every word is meaningful.

Original story	Note
Soon, with the help of the fire department, and according to the appropriate protocol, the patient was removed from the wreckage. She was awake throughout the rescue operation. She had been provided with infusion and a neck support. She was lifted out of the wreck and was immobilised on a stretcher by laying her down on a vacuum mattress. Subsequently, as we were pushing the stretcher into the ambulance, the patient who was awake all the time, but did not say a word, quietly and curiously asked, *"Did you put me to sleep? When did you get me out?"* In fact, this was the point when I realised that I had not even given her any of the already prepared medications.	In accordance with the suggestions given earlier, the injured "awakens" as she is being wheeled to the ambulance. In the state of trance, the patient's reality-orientation gets distorted, which is natural in such situations (she does not know whether she was anesthetised or not).
The patient's care took place according to the rules hereinafter, and although she showed signs of some chest pain when hitting bumps during her transportation, she described it as "Now I feel it again, of course it's not as intense as it was earlier in the car. Now I feel it much less, but it still hurts." She didn't mention shortness of breath any more.	The pain from the injury is in the "acceptable" zone. She feels the bumps in accordance with the actual situation. In this case, it is a good idea to establish suggestions for the future that pain is a useful signal, for it is a message of the body (for example, it is worthwhile to project forward for the period of recuperation: the most likely message is that for regeneration of the body, rest and tranquility are required).

Initial situation	Goal
– Negative trance – Pain, agitation	– To neutralise negative trance – Establish compliance – To calm both body and soul – Analgesia

DESCRIBER OF THE CASE: Csaba Diószeghy Dr., Anesthesiologist-Intensive Therapy, Oxycologist-Emergency Specialist.

THE FIRST EDITION: Varga K., Diószeghy Cs. (2001) *Hűtésbefizetés, avagy a szuggesztiók szerepe a mindennapi orvosi gyakorlatban.* /Cooling fee, or suggestions' role in the everyday medical practice/ Pólya Kiadó, Budapest, 49. oldal.

Adenosine

Original story	Note
The other day, a lady was admitted to the hospital with heart problems. Having seen her electrocardiography (ECG), I told the junior doctor that they could start her on adenosine[5]. The lady was lying on the bed in peace, on the infusion and on the monitor. Everybody is peaceful and relaxed. Then the junior doctor steps up to her with an ampoule of adenosine in his hand. I could overhear their conversation: "I will give you medication which will hopefully return your pace to normal. As I inject it, you will feel quite awful, as if you were about to faint, but don't worry, you won't. In addition to this, you may feel unbearable pain, which is quite unpleasant. However, this is still the best medication we have and since your heart beats too fast, we need to stop it for a while." I could not see the lady's face, but having heard this conversation, I started to walk over to them… Just then, the medication was plumped in… The lady screamed and turned gray. She snatched at her chest and grabbed on to it, hardly breathing. She squealed that she cannot breathe and will die. Of course she did not. However, despite all of this, her pace did not return to normal. I got there. Unfortunately in this case, we have to repeat the injection and double the dose.	The young colleague's 'informing' is a prototype for negative suggestions: – Conveys doubt: 'hopefully returns.' – 'Prescribes' negative side effects: you will feel awful, as if you were about to faint, you may feel unbearable pain in the chest, unpleasant. – Contains negativity 'don't worry, you won't.' – Makes the whole intervention appear doubtful: 'this is still the best medication we have.' – For the laypeople, it formulates a catastrophic aim: her heart needs to be stopped. Of course all this takes an effect.

5 (The original author's note:) Adenosine needs to be injected when a certain pace problem occurs. One of the quite unpleasant side effects is that it may

Original story	Note
"Well, this was almost perfect! However, it seems to me that you will need another dose for full results. Did you feel the medication taking an effect?" She looks at me doubtfully.	The 'opening' is surprising (**taking over rapport**): instead of failure, the doctor labels the situation 'almost perfect' (**reframing**). 'Did you feel the medication taking an effect' he escalates the surprise even more. Of course she did. This time the doctor links this experience with a pleasant (and desirable) outcome (medication taking an effect).
"Are you feeling all right now?" "Yes, I am okay."	The list of questions draws the patient into an active interaction (note this below as well). This plays an important role in **maintaining rapport** too: pay attention here but not anywhere else, and especially not to the junior doctor. This method may become useful when trying to prevent the patient from other's negative suggestions.
"Isn't it unusual that this medication only has an effect for a couple of seconds, and yet has such strong long-term impact? These new medications are indeed wonderful!" The lady looks at me even more doubtfully and mistrustfully than before.	The still weird questions reinforce the effectiveness of the medication again (**repetition**). At the same time, they convey facts (**yes-set**).

---

cause faint-like symptoms for a couple of seconds and sometimes pain in the chest. However, adenosine breaks down so quickly that it only takes effect for a brief 9–15 seconds. Therefore, any unpleasant side effect disappears within seconds, and during this time, pace mostly returns to normal.
Every description contains this unpleasant side effect. Doctors are recommended to warn the patient. However, they do not describe how to do this. When I teach, I always tell *how* and I explain how to reframe side effects for the patient. I myself use this medication quite often and I always discuss it with the patient. I have never ever seen anyone complain when being injected or complain about this bloody unpleasant experience… Contrary to this: they sometimes mention (quite happily!) that they can indeed feel the medication taking an effect and how wonderful this is!

Original story	Note
"*It can indeed be a little scary if someone doesn't know what to expect. But best of all is that you can really feel as though your heart beat returns to normal. It is a strange feeling, isn't it?*" "It was rather painful."	The 'little scary' desensitises (**reframing**) the patient's experience, at the same time, describes her feeling (**pacing**). This is followed by another advantage which prospects **positivity** ('the best of all', **implication**). This is where the key suggestion comes, which has been prepared by the previous suggestions (**leading**): your heart rate returns to normal. Another **reframing** which desensitises the experience even further, from 'scary' into 'strange'.
"*Really? Most patients say that it is like a push and they can indeed feel their heart rate return to normal. Of course everyone can have a different experience, but what they have in common is that it only lasts for a couple of seconds, like it did in your case.*" "Oh yes."	The patient's complaint is surprisingly received by giving an immediate reason for it: quoting other patients' description (**anecdotes, modelling**). Another **reframing** of possible sensations: push-like, which is followed by the **repetition** of the expected effect: the heart rate returns to normal. Although 'everyone can have a different experience,' the effect, as said in black and white, will only lasts for a couple of seconds (**direct suggestion**).
"*So it is probably best if we repeat the injection since it seems that your heart reacts very well. Sometimes three doses are needed to return the heart rate to normal; however, in your case, I think there is a high chance that only two will be needed.*" "Well..." (she does not seem very happy about it). "Okay. You know what to do."	This is where the doctor comes up with the idea of the new (double) dose. Note the phrase 'we' and the tentative suggestion to draw the patient into the decision (**providing a sense of control**). Two compared to three doses 'desensitises' the effect. The activity is common (return) and the target suggestion is again **repeated** (normal heart rate).

Original story	Note
"*Yes, I do know. So would you be so kind as to observe if you feel anything unusual how short it lasts: six or rather nine seconds? I will keep my eye on the screen to watch your heart rate. All right?*" "All right," answers the lady confidently.	Now the doctor undoubtedly takes on the role of being competent (**direct suggestion**). The possible 'unusual feeling' (**reframing, repetition**) is drawn into a **double-bind:** six or nine seconds. The patient is given the task of observing 'externally' (**dissociative strategy**).
Following this, I inject the second (double) dose. The lady sat without a sound. The heart rate returned to normal.	

Initial situation	Goal
– Frightened patient, complaining about extreme physical symptoms. – Colleague giving negative suggestions – New dose is necessary	– Dismiss scared feelings – Take over rapport and establish cooperation and trust – Rebalance negative suggestions

DESCRIBER OF THE CASE: Csaba Diószeghy, Dr., Anesthesiologist-Intensive Therapy, Oxycologist-Emergency Specialist.

THE FIRST EDITION: Diószeghy Csaba (2006) Van egy jópofa eset. / There is a good fellow case/ *Hipno-Info, 2006 őszi szám*, 135–136. oldal.

Tractor

Original story	Note
We were preparing for a magnetic resonance imaging (MRI) examination under anaesthesia. The examination is only successful if our little patient lies completely still and calm during the procedure. In the case of children, this is a lot more difficult to achieve as they have to overcome their fear of the unknown, and the outer world must be fully excluded: the machine gives out a strong, loud, and clattering noise during the examination. The situation is further complicated by the fact that the child has to stay in a room all alone until the examination is over. Ferike is seven years old and is mentally retarded. This is another reason why anaesthesia was indicated, "as he cannot possibly stay still for eight to ten minutes"	
Approaching the conclusion of the previous MRI, I went to the waiting room and called for Ferike, waiting there with his mother. *"I'm looking for Ferike P."* "We are here." I introduced myself to the mother and I told her that it would soon be their turn. I crouched down to the little boy and we shook hands.	The **rapport** building starts out with the professional going to the waiting room, instead of waiting for the patient in the unknown, fierce examination place, behind the door (**pacing**). Contact is made with the mother, then with the little boy. The serious manly gesture of shaking hands is the symbol of **cooperation**. The physical touch itself puts down the foundations for a trusting relationship.

Original story	Note
"Hello Ferike, I'm Zsolt. I'm here to help you through the examination. I'll make sure that everything goes alright... Do you want to know what will happen?" "Yes," he answered confidently; an unexpected reaction for me. *"Alright, then we will take a look together with mommy. Come in."*	The details of rapport building are important: in this case, the first name is enough (the title and the likes would probably only be confusing). The opening sentence determines the framework of **cooperation** and the outcome: the child receives help; everything will be alright (**positivity**). So that nothing would go wrong. The child is indeed curious about the procedure, so taking a look at the machine is a practical solution (**giving a sense of control**). All this takes place with the mother present (transferring **rapport** is gradual), but it can be felt that the professional controls things.
We go inside confidently, but he stops short at the huge door of the examination room. He stares at the huge machine. *"Come and we will take a closer look at it!"* *"This is a camera, a very-very big camera. It is the biggest one we have here,"* I say. Then I reach out my hand... and though he is a bit shy, he takes my hand.	The professional senses the insecurity of the child and reacts at once: by adjusting to the knowledge level of the child, he calls the machine a 'big camera' (**reframing**). The child accepts the professional's reaching hand. This must have been enabled by their earlier "routine-like" handshake. These are tiny but important steps, so that the child clinging to his mother would be willing to stay alone during the examination. It is important that the professional observe how "prepared" the child is for being alone in the machine, cut off from his mother.

Original story	**Note**
"See, here is where the photos are made and you have to lie here until they are all done. Well, it does not seem that difficult, right? Maybe you were a bit more nervous up until now, but really, this is all that it is about."	While explaining the machine, taking photos comes up again (reframing, repetition). There is a **yes-set** consisting of three elements hidden in the explanation (See (1) here is where the photos are made (2), and you have to lie here until then (3), and well, it does not seem that difficult, right (**goal centering**). The nervousness because the situation is already in past tense and it becomes more and more clear how simple it is.
It seems to me that he has become a bit more relaxed. He walks up to his mom. I step closer: *"I know that you have come for an examination with anaesthesia, but there is another alternative."* I crouch and turn to Ferike. *"We can do it in another way, much faster, and you don't even have to go sleep. This way you could go home sooner, and at the end of the examination, there would be a present for YOU!"*	As the professional senses how well he can cooperate with the child, he offers a simpler alternative to the mother and later describes its details to the little boy: The features of the alternative without anaesthesia, they'll get home faster and there is also a present, are obviously attractive for a child (**motivating, positivity**). The present itself is connected to the end of the examination, but it is already envisaged now: with this implying that the examination will come to an end all right (**future orientation**).
"We have a huge box full of toys. People working here have collected them for similar boys like you." "A present?" His eyes open wide. I show him the box and its contents. *"Boys who HAVE DONE A GOOD JOB can choose a toy from this box."*	What is more, the presents are shown in their own reality, increasing their attraction (**object suggestions**), and the earlier (linked to them) suggestion becomes a concrete certainty: the examination will take place without any problem. Those who "have done a good job" can choose from this: in an **implied** way, but evidently conveys the message that you will also do a good job and thus you can choose a toy, too (**modelling, repetition, future orientation**).

Original story	Note
"I tell you Ferike, what you'll have to do." "O.K." And we are already heading toward the machine. *"Lie down on this examination table. The most important thing is that you stay still until I tell you that you can move. Shall we do it?"* "Yes." And he is already climbing up on the table.	After such a preparation, the child will be much more open and motivated for the instructions given here. The question "shall we do it?" invites **cooperation** and immediately generates the answer.
"Ferike, while the photos are being taken, you will hear a loud, rattling noise like a tractor… Do not let it bother you. But perhaps it will be easier that while you are in the camera, you pretend that you are mowing the grass in a garden with a noisy tractor. He simply nods, "O.K".	The information given beforehand on what to expect offers a neutral and even positive (playful) framework for interpretation (**reframing**), which the child accepts.
Now an unexpected thing happens. "Can't mommy come here beside me?" he asks shyly. His mother is obviously expecting a baby. In her condition, it is not at all recommended to stay here during the examination. *"Mommy is taking care of your baby sibling, who is still in her tummy. She cannot come in now."*	The mother has to stay outside: the professional shares the real (!) cause for this with the child. Notice that his wording is positive throughout. He does not say "No, she cannot come in", but only says the noble reason behind this (**informing**).

Original story	Note
"Do you think it would help if I stayed here and hold your foot during the examination?" "That'd be good!"	The professional immediately offers his own presence and (repeated) touch: starting from the handshake, these touches are more and more important. Though the offer is phrased as a question, it has strong suggestive power – especially if it is pronounced with an intonation that is similar to an affirmative sentence: "it would help you..." (**positivity**) You are not going to throw a tantrum, right?
"Then lie down, make yourself comfy, and put your head on this pillow." The MRI assistant steps up to me and there is a scaffold to be placed over the head. This needs to be put over Lacika's head. "*Now Ferike, this is like a space helmet. This makes the photos really nice. Close your eyes softly, relaxed! Meanwhile, I'll hold your feet as I promised.*"	The further accessories of the examination are introduced with the help of pictures (**reframing**), from which it is easy to choose from for the child (photo, tractor, space helmet). The information provided is **positive**, all along (comfortably, the picture will be nice, softly, relaxed). You mustn't move, because then all is in vain.
The examination begins... difficult moments... Will he get scared from the loud noise? Will he be able to stay perfectly still? And there is only a few seconds' pause (silence) between the "photos", and I also have to concentrate on not asking him questions in case he would start nodding or moving automatically.	In the seemingly passive period, the professional's attention focuses on the child, maintains being attuned while all this is conveyed toward the child through continuous touching.

Original story	Note
During the few seconds' breaks between frames: *"You are doing a good job. As you can hear, the tractor has started... Pay attention only to mowing the grass everywhere. We are doing great here. You have mowed the grass in more than half of the yard. Just keep it up, buddy. Now comes the next turn. We're almost done."* In ten minutes, we are done. The examination is over.	The professional also maintains a continuous verbal **rapport**. He uses the already introduced pictures to inform him that everything is going according to plan. The wording of all this underlines the child's braveness and the mutual success (**positivity, giving a sense of control**).
"Ferike, congratulations, you did a good job. Come and choose a present for yourself." He dumps the whole box, and after a lengthy search, he chooses something for himself. He happily brings it to his mom.	He deserves the promised present.
I did not think that this little boy would be able to go through this procedure. I was afraid that he would not succeed. *"He did a really good job. He is capable of a lot more than you would think."*	The successful procedure is a highlighted result, along with the examination result....
We say goodbye. Ferike turns back from the door waving goodbye with a smile: "Goodbye!"	

Initial situation	Goal
– The child who is attached to his mother and presumably is afraid of the examination	– Establishing report and compliance – Positive reframing of the situation – Establishing a relaxed bodily position for the examination

DESCRIBER OF THE CASE: Zsolt Benedek, Anesthesiological Assistant.

THE FIRST EDITION: Exam paper for the postgraduate training program on Suggestive Communication in Somatic Medicine, co-organised by the Hungarian Association of Hypnosis and Semmelweis University School of Medicine, Budapest.

Medication

Original story	Note[6]
One day I was called to a consultation. This is always an exciting and challenging opportunity to improvise a mental health check and intervention in the company of doctors and assistants of other specialties. A patient on the otolaryngology unit became agitated and defensive the day after his gland operation for cancer. In an irritated manner, he told the doctor in charge that people in the corridor constantly talk about him and laugh at him. As he understood, they want to put him on the internet to become a subject of further bullying. He declared that he will no longer stay in the hospital (which would put him at risk) and he demanded to see his own doctor right then and there (unfortunately, his doctor was abroad that time). He refused the follow-up examination and he rejected his medication, including the tranquiliser. Within half an hour, I was with him as the doctor-in-charge.	

6 Initial remarks of the original author are also used in the text.

Original story	Note
When I entered the patient's room, along with a colleague and a nurse, he stood by the window and stared at the street. Frightened, he looked at us, stepped back a little, and faced us. Moving calmly, I stepped forward, reached out for his hand, greeted him, and introduced myself. Still looking scared, he accepted my hand and rushed an introduction. He was visibly very agitated and perhaps seriously frightened as well.	The patient's behaviour unmistakably shows signs of negative trance. This entry of new doctors undoubtedly reflects that there are new members of the patient's treatment team (although this is not favourable regarding rapport, it reflects reality). In this situation, it is especially important to show precisely the elements of reality to the patient. The new doctor on the scene starts to peacefully build rapport by offering his hand (**implication, non-verbal suggestion**). The patient accepts the hand. This is the first sign of his cooperation. Do not be nervous!
"*The doctor asked me to visit you,* I started, *to see if I could help you. I was told you have unpleasant feelings and you would like to leave the clinic.*" "And what do you want here? What do you want?"	This is according to reality; the doctor avoids the word 'examine' (**informing**). 'If I could help you' defines the situation and suggests acceptance of medical help. Judging from before, he addresses the patient on the level where the patient currently is (**pacing**). Despite all this, the patient is dismissive and obnoxious.
"*Would you allow me to sit down?*" I asked. Then I placed a chair near the visibly uncertain, anxious, agitated, and untrusting patient with a slow and calm movement. I sat down and waited for a couple of moments. There was another chair next to him. *"I would like us to find the best solution,"* I told him and signaled at the same time that he may sit down as well. He sat down.	The rhythm, the pause, and the asymmetric body position reinforce the friendly approach (**repetition, implication**). By the arrangement of furniture, the doctor sets an excellent example of **object suggestions.** The wording offers **cooperation** (i.e. using 'us'). The 'best solution' suggests that there are other possible solutions and all they have to do is choose (**positive implication, giving a sense of control**). Alongside the words, gestures also play an important role in the communication (**nonverbal suggestion**). This also serves as a fine 'leading' of the patient (**attempt to lead**). The fact that the patient takes the seat is a positive indication that he accepts the doctor's approach.

Original story	Note
"Are you now recording what I'm saying?" He wants to know (I can feel it from his voice that he is afraid I might be). "*Unfortunately, I did not bring a recorder. Would you like it if I did record the conversation?*" "No, I would not," he says relieved.	The surprising answer (**paradox suggestion**) reassures the patient that the doctor does not use a tape recorder and that he has nothing to be afraid of.
"*I can see there is still a bandage and a drain on your neck. Have you just had an operation?*" "Yes." "*Yesterday?*" "Yes." "*Were you asleep during the procedure?*" "Yes I was." "*It seems to me that the operation was successful. Do you have any pain now?*" "No, I don't." "*Where do you live? Where are you from, by the way?*" "Do you really want to interrogate me about everything now?"	Listing obvious facts is the beginning of a **yes-set** as well as a tool to keep the patient in interaction (**building of rapport**). The rejecting answer to the last question suggests that the patient's patience has its limits of cooperation.
"*Not about everything. I know for example when you were born.*" "How do you know that?" "*It is tattooed on your hand.*" "Yeah, it is." "*I can also see that you are anxious, suspicious, and nervous. You feel uncomfortable and you wonder if I could indeed help you.*"	Reading the year of birth from the tattoo refers first to the doctors 'supernatural' skills. He 'plays with fire' as this act insinuates for a moment that without his consent, the doctor may know a lot of things about the patient. The rational explanation of the tattoo provides a sense of relief and it decreases paranoia. This is immediately followed by naming the patient's anxiety and nervousness (**pacing**). The phrase "you wonder if I could indeed help you" is another attempt to have the patient accept help (**implication**).

Original story	Note
"You would also be nervous if everyone talked about you." *"You mean, you can hear in here what they're saying about you out in the corridor?"* "Yes. And the visitors laugh at me all the time too. I've had enough of it." *"This must be a terrible feeling indeed."* "Now you think I'm just making it up."	This question ("you mean, you can hear in here...") is an attempt to clarify the patient's problem. It is another step of **pacing** and further suggests that the doctor is taking the patient's complaint seriously and that he would like to understand exactly what is going on. The doctor's response ("this must be a terrible feeling indeed") is full of empathy. Only after this statement do the first vague signs appear that the patient may actually consider his experience to be questionable.
"*I think you really feel what you feel and you can't get better here under such uncomfortable circumstances. Now I understand why you thought of going home. Have you had any visitors?*"	Another empathic response (**empathy**) by the doctor may convey that there is someone here already who understands the patient (**pacing**).
"No, I haven't had any." "*Can they be expected to come?*" "My son and his family live far away..." "*So you are left alone in this situation. I think you are somewhat uncertain as what to do now....*"	The doctor's new series of empathic responses further deepen the patient's trust.
"You know, I am completely unsure..."	And here comes the patient's first open and honest sentence.
"*I completely understand. It would be great to get rid of this unpleasant feeling, wouldn't it?* "Yes." *"I think we have medication for this kind of anxiety..."*	Following the acceptance of the newest empathic response, the doctor tries the medication card. This move may be a bit too hasty and a bit too radical. It immediately triggers resistance.
"You wanna hit me with a sack of medication?" "*Nurse,*" I turn to the assistant, "*do we have a sack of medication here?*" "No, we don't, doctor," she answers.	The doctor's reaction serves as a fine source of humour as well as draws the staff in. It is also an attempt to expand trust. Luckily, the nurse 'gets the picture'.

Original story	Note
"But you must have two pills of Haloperidol, don't you? Please bring the box too, and only open it here, so that I can see..."	The artificial mistrust fits well with the patient's attitude (**pacing**).
Then I noticed the patient's glass on the nightstand. *"Do you have a glass?"* "Yes, I do." *"Would you like some tea or would you rather get some water from the tap for yourself?"*	The words 'tea or water' are negligible details aiming to get him to take the medication (**double-bind, implication**).
The patient started to walk towards the tap. Without any hesitation he accepted and swallowed the pill. *"Did it go down smoothly?"* I finally asked. "Yes, I swallowed it."	
"All right, then we'll ask the doctor now, who is after all the expert in this, to check if the pill may have gotten stuck on your tonsils... Good. Shortly you will feel relieved and I hope your unpleasant feelings will go away."	Following the successful administration of the medicine, it is time to **transfer the rapport** to the colleague. The doctor mediates fortunate outcomes regarding the future (**leading, positivity, future orientation**).
"Would you allow me to visit you tomorrow?"	The question offers choice and superficially transfers **control**, since the answer is predictable from the previous interaction.
"As you wish, doctor" he replied.	

Initial situation	Goal
– Suspicious and agitated patient – No cooperation with the initial otolaryngology staff	– Build cooperation – Avoid acute psychiatric hospitalisation

DESCRIBER OF THE CASE: Zoltán Ambrus Kovács Dr., Psychiatrist.

THE FIRST EDITION: Varga K. (ed.) (2011) Beyond the words. Communication and suggestion in medical practice. Nova Science Publisher, New York.

Stroke

Original story	Note
A 76-year-old widow is taken to the emergency department by ambulance. The examinations showed she had had an acute ischemic stroke. Due to the elevated level of glucose in the blood, she was initially treated at the diabetes department and then because of the decline in her status, she was taken to the neuro-intensive unit led by me.	
At her admission we saw a poorly developed and nurtured, exhausted, massively acetonic, pale, hypothermic, and incurable-looking elderly woman, who had her eyes and lips tightly shut. The ambulance personnel laid her on the bed. The nurses took her clothes off right away, then they put the EKG electrodes on which showed a very rapid heartbeat. They put the blood pressure monitor on her left upper arm. It showed low blood pressure. The oxygen probe was put in her nose and she was given oxygen at three litres per minute. She had some peripheral vein through which a physiological saline was dripping. Nurses noticed that her right limbs were immobile. The swallowing test was carried out by squirting a couple of drops of water in her mouth. She choked right away, so they wanted to administer a stomach tube. To this she said screaming, "I won't allow this!" This is when I got there and stood at her left side.	

Original story	Note
I introduced myself and told her that I would be her physician and that we would help her. I asked her what I might call her. She didn't answer. I kept on going: "*Can I call you Marika?*" She didn't answer. "*I would like to examine you,*" I continued. Then she turned her head fixed to the right, a little bit towards me, opened her eyes, and started to speak dysarthrically (because of a right side central facial paresis): "No! Just leave me alone! Go away! Don't do anything on me! Just leave me, I want to die…" "Oh, you can't say such a thing, Marika" interrupted one of the nurses.	The doctor gets in contact starting with introducing herself (**rapport**). If you do not cooperate, we can't help
I asked for a blanket, wrapped her in it, and asked to be left alone. "*If you want to die you will. No one can stop you,*" I said.	The expert builds **rapport** with the gesture of wrapping her in a blanket and by ensuring privacy. With this she conveys that something different is coming and that the treatment will not go on in the previous manner. In the new phase, her opening statement: "if you want to die you will", is almost provocative. It doesn't just rhyme with the patient's previous statement that she wanted to die (**pacing**), but it is also an awareness-raising opening. She ensures the patient that no one is to stop her here.
She looked at me and for a second the left corner of her mouth curved upward. She closed her eyes.	The patient's small but significant signals show the forming of the **rapport**.
Then I took off my gloves and I carefully put my left palm on her chest. She didn't pull away (the monitor showed a 33 respiration rate).	The taking off of the gloves is another sophisticated sign of 'something new' coming (**rapport**). The fact that the patient accepts the doctor's touch and does not pull away is another favorable sign that she is o.k. with such connection.

Original story	Note
I waited around for five minutes with my hand resting on her chest and I didn't say a word.	Doing nothing and knowing how to wait are important parts of solving tough situations. They keep pressing on the doctor's intention to help, to be patient, and to adjust to the patient's needs.
She warmed up from the blanket and she got used to my hand. Then tenderly, according to the rhythm of her breathing, I applied pressure on her chest and started slowing her breathing, during which I still didn't say anything. About ten minutes may have passed. Now the monitor showed a 20-count respiration rate and her pulse also slowed down.	
Then quietly and slowly I asked: "*Marika, do you have a garden?*" "Yes I do." "*Do you plant flowers?*" "Yes." "*Marika, do you have grandchildren?*" "Yes." "*And do you love them?*" "Yes." "*Would you like to see them again?*" "…Yes." "*I would like to help you to make it possible. Will you let me?*" "…Yes." "*You have two kids, right?*" "Yes." "*And your son found you, right?*" "Yes." "*Did you come here by ambulance?*" "Yes." "*You see that you are safe here, right?*" "Yes." "*Will you let me examine you?*" "…Yes."	After such a dismal start, the resigned patient who just wanted to die now answers questions that have nothing to do with the situation, about flowers and grandchildren. The **'yes-set'** that unfolds in connection with the questions sets the ground to what's coming next. First, the key suggestion "I would like to help you with this, will you let me?" gets a confirmation from the patient, by which it's defined that this is about helping her, and she accepts this help (**rapport**). This is where the phase that was prepared by following turns into **leading**. In the second half of the **'yes-set'**, within the just achieved cooperation, they make it clear that there will be an examination, but this time with the consent of the patient (**rapport**). Mentioning of family members (kids and grandchildren) raises the **motivation** for recovery and at the same time, by mentioning the chance of reunion, it opens a positive perspective (**future orientation**).

Original story	Note
I examined her. The results were worse than I expected. She was seriously dehydrated and smelled of acetone. I found out that her sugar level was 16 mmol/l. She had probably lost a lot of weight lately. She may have been very weak even before the stroke. On her right side, she lost her vision, had facial nerve paralysis, and was nearly fully paralysed, with pathologically vivid reflexes. I didn't notice any serious sensational difficulties. She couldn't swallow. But she was able to speak, with some dysarthria; she understood everything addressed to her, reacted adequately, was clearly conscious, and was oriented in all respects. However, she was probably depressed. She was protecting her stomach. It was sensitive to pressure all over. She wasn't able to hold her urine.	
"Marika, it looks like you got diabetes and you have had a stroke, but together we can improve both conditions by a lot. First, the blood sugar needs to be stabilised and mobility has to be restored on your right side. It's enough for today, and tomorrow we will take another step forward. When is the last time you had anything to eat or drink?"	The doctor factually informs the patient about the results of the examination (**informing**), emphasising the possibilities right away and underlining the importance of cooperation: "together we can improve ...by a lot" (**rapport**). She makes a plan right away, defining the daily **goal** and outlining that the next day there will be other things to do (**future orientation**).
"Well, I don't even know... I also threw up at home. Nothing feels good anymore since my husband died." *"It must be hard to be alone. Luckily you have your kids and grandchildren."* *"Yes, yes..."*	The patient voices her grief and pain, to which the doctor briefly reacts (empathic answer, **pacing**), but quickly refers to the family bonds that are functioning well (**positivity, future orientation**).

Original story	Note
"*Swallowing would be hard now. Until you get better, I will lead a thin, soft tube through your nose and into your stomach so that we can feed you to get you stronger quickly.*" "I will not allow that! My husband died after a gastroscopy. No, no, I will not allow that. If I have rights, I will not allow it!"	The patient refuses the proposed intervention. Luckily the reason is revealed right away: her husband died in connection with a gastroscopy (**negative modeling**).
I asked for a stomach tube. I unwrapped it right before her eyes. She turned her head away and closed her eyes. I put her left hand in mine. She didn't pull it away.	The patient does not want to see the tube, but the doctor successfully uses the previously worked tactile modality.
"*Marika, this is not a gastroscopy, like your husband had. You had a stroke so you have swallowing difficulties. Well, you can't starve to death, right? Look at it, feel how thin and soft this tube is.? Like a piece of straw.*" She opened her eyes just a crack and then closed it. "*Hold it! We will not put it in by force, I promise,*" I said. Then I put the tube in her left hand. She was feeling it, touching it. "I don't want it," she declared, isn't there any other solution?"	With factual informing, the doctor tries to lead the patient from a false interpretation to the right one (**informing, reframing**). Her reasoning "you can't starve to death" is built on basic motives (**motivating**). The patient is dismissing with words, but by her touch and her opening of her eyes a little, she shows that she is orienting herself, by the wish of the doctor. Instead of the total dismissal, she is more constructive: the question "Isn't there any other solution?" show that she understands the goal, but its method is unacceptable for her.

Original story	Note
"Not for now. But I can tell you that other patients who got this tube and had been very afraid of it, told me afterwards that had they known it was so easily administered, they wouldn't have been so scared. Of course we give everyone anesthesia, and if you want, we can even put you to sleep for a minute."	The doctor's answer is seemingly negative "not for now", but it also hints on future alternate possibilities (**implication, future orientation**). Instead of the negative model of her husband's case, the doctor brings up other patients as **positive models**, and by referring to their fears, she shows the patient that she understands her feelings (empathic answer, **pacing**). She quickly continues clarifying the details, as if the decision has already been made about the main question (whether or not using a tube), and the only question remaining was the usage of anesthesia (**double bind**).
"No, I don't want my head to be bleary. And when will you take it out?"	The patient does not want anesthesia and she already inquires about taking the tube out: her perspective became future-oriented.
"I hope in a couple of days, if you get stronger and your swallowing gets better, or we find a better solution. So, will you let me spray the analgesic into your nose? Which one of your nostrils do you prefer?" "The left one…"	The doctor's answer is a suggestion outlining the **goal** (you get stronger and your swallowing gets better). Like the previous steps, this intervention is up to the patient's consent, by letting her choose the side of her nose (**double-bind**).
The tube slid down easily. Having this done, she easily gave permission to have the central line (I put her to sleep for it), and the bladder catheter administered. We were giving insulin by perfusion. She was getting liquids and ions and her blood pressure was artificially raised. We were administering the special formula for diabetics in gradually increased doses. As her physiological signs were getting better and stabilised, she got languid and fell asleep.	

Original story	Note
The next day, by the time of the first rounds, my patient was awake and looking around in a 30 degree panorama in a raised sitting position. When she saw me she smiled, and she recognised me. By then her physiological parameters were within normal range. I asked her to raise her right arm, then her right leg. To my surprise, she performed pretty well, but then she suddenly dropped her leg and said, "No, no, I can't do it". "*But this is really good! You have improved a lot already. You'll see, with every day, in all aspects, you will get better and better. With every day, in all aspects, you will get better and better,*" I repeated.	The open appreciation of the actual "performance" helps the realistic evaluation of the situation while confidently outlining the potential improvement (**positivity, future orientation**). The repeated key-suggestion (**repetition**): "with every day, in all aspects, you will get better and better" gives space to consider the possible outcome of that improvement (**implication**).

Initial situation	Goal
– Dismissal and hostile patient	– Building cooperation – Building motivation for recovery

DESCRIBER OF THE CASE: Katalin Judit Tóth Dr., Anesthesiologist, Intensive Care Specialist, Pediatrician and Pediatric Neurologist.

THE FIRST EDITION: Tóth Katalin Judit (2008) Szuggesztiós terápia lehetőségei a neurointenzív ellátás során. /Suggestive therapy's possibilities in the neurointensive care/ *Hipno-Info, 2008 tavaszi szám*, 18–23. oldal.

Brave Man

Original story	Note
A 28-year-old mentally disabled young man had to have a tissue growth removed from his face. The ear nose and thorax (ENT) clinic sent the patient to the surgery department. They believed the surgery could be carried out with local anaesthesia. It could have happened, but not even three people in the surgery department could hold the young man down. He was very scared and could only think about himself being hurt. He could not be soothed, so the idea of general anaesthesia came up as a possible solution.	Negative trance is obvious: the patient most assuredly doesn't understand what is happening to him, he's afraid of unknown situations and people, and he's acting accordingly to his feelings. Violence (holding him down) doesn't work; another solution has to be found.
This would be fine, but how could we make him come into the operating room and lie down on the operating table? Then it occurred to the ear-nose-throat colleague that I had for a long time been assisting with the task of administering anesthesia for people living with down syndrome or mental disabilities in the oral surgery clinic. That is how it happened that the mother and son contacted me while riding in our hospital's anesthesiology ambulance.	The doctor's previous experiences create the possibility of managing the challenging task of administering general anesthesia to the young man (to whom this would be an unknown and frightening experience similar to the previously failed local anesthesia). It is important to recognise that the young man had already had a negative experience related to the medical situation. Moreover, the disappointment (i.e. coming from his family) about the former failure was also transmitted to him.
The young man sat with his head bent down, holding his mother's hand. They were sitting in that position by the desk while the mother explained in a few words that she realised that the lump on his son's face was disturbing him and that he kept saying it was sore. They came for sorting this problem out and suggested that the operation should involve general anesthesia.	The patient obviously has good **rapport** with his mother – he could be "won" for anesthesia from that close bond. Of course, in this case, the mother is not simply an attendant: everything that is going to happen will be mediated to the patient through the mother's feelings too.

Original story	Note
"Hi Dénes, I'm the anesthesiologist, and now we are going to play a game. Only things that you too agree with are going to happen. Do you see this thing in my hand? It is called a stethoscope. We are going to listen how your heart says lub-dub, lub-dub, and you are going to take a deep breath, and then blow it out. I am going to listen to what your lungs tell me. Can we start? Can I listen?"	Taking up the **rapport** is a mixture of the communication of facts and **direct suggestions.** An important promise is said at the very beginning (only things that you too agree with are going to happen), in which the word "too" **implies** cooperation. The doctor clarifies in advance what she is about to do in a way that it can be understandable to the young man (**informing**), hiding the goal suggestion in the facts (**yes-set**): we are going to listen. In the latter, the use of first person plural refers to cooperation (**repetition**). The doctor, indeed, asks for permission to start the simple procedure, just as she has promised before (giving a **sense of control**).
I'm smiling, looking into his eyes, and caressing his left soulder as I'm speaking. Meanwhile, the young man holds his mother's hands in his hands.	The doctor's nonverbal signals tell him about her helpful intentions and that he can feel safe on a more basic level than her words indicate. The "hand on the shoulder" is a direct physical contact that will reemerge in the story several times again. This gesture has "no function", in a sense that it is not an inevitable part of an examination like this. It is an element of the emotional channel through which the main messages of "calmness" and "safety" are mediated. However, the patient indicates, by holding his mother's hands, that she is still the main source of safety for him.

Original story	**Note**
The examination could successfully be carried out. I complimented him for doing so well and for behaving so excellently. During this, he already let go of his mother's hands, facing me. He was rewarded with a spatula, which he accepted and tookfrom my hands.	The examination was successfully done. Letting go of the mother's hands must have been a goal commonly reached by mother and son. Seeing the new doctor's understanding communication after the previous failures must have been relaxing for the mother, so she could mediate her own calmness to her son: "you are surely safe here, I can trust this doctor with you." The young man turns to the doctor. The **rapport** deepens.
The following step was pulse oximetry. First, I put the "clip" on my own 'pointing finger' on my left hand and we listened to the rhythmical sound and watched the numbers and the waves on the screen together. Then I made an offer, now we'll put it on your finger and we'll see what sound it makes.	The doctor demonstrates the pulse oximeter's use on her own hand (**modeling**), and by doing so, she shows that everything that happens is simple, understandable, and harmless. They watch the screen together, which shows the cooperation again (giving a **sense of control**).
I asked him: Would you put the clip on your finger or shall I do it? He looked at his mother, who encouraged him, but finally, he turned his head away and leant it on his mother's shoulder. She embraced him. He didn't dare take the clip, so I asked: "can I put it on your finger?" I didn't get any answer, so I took off the clip and put it on his left hand's pointing finger.	The doctor makes an offer about the clip in **double-bind**. The young man backs off. Seeking a closer physical contact with his mother probably means that it is too much for him. However, the doctor does not stop, although she can sense these signs. Interpreting the lack of any answer as the patient's unwillingness to put the clip on by himself, she does it instead of him (as it was indicated by one of the variations of **double-bind**), though she asks for his permission for doing so (giving a **sense of control**).
He stiffened, did not react, did not move, or protest, and the pulse oximeter made a sound, it started clicking rhythmically, according to the frequency of his pulse.	The young man stiffened, but luckily he did not protest.

Original story	Note
I put my hand on his left shoulder and stroked it, I complimented him for being so brave and doing so well, and told him to listen to the sound with me because it is given by his heart.	The "hand put on the shoulder" indicates another successful step, which is followed by a **repeated** compliment.
I told the assistant (who was sitting in front of the computer silently, almost invisibly, not turning around or asking questions, just staring at the screen in silence): O2 sat: 98%, pulse: 96.	The assistant is a great help in building the **rapport** by doing her job passively. This way, the patient's attention could turn only to his mother and the doctor, and there is no other "source of attack" he should monitor.
From that point on, he allowed me to take his blood pressure, RR: 110/70 Hgmm. Then I opened up my mouth as widely as I could and said "AAAAAAA", and asked him: *"Let's say together, AAAAAAAA!"* And he said 'aah', so I could observe his mouth opening (norm), the visibility of the pharyngeal bend (Mallampati: I). This examination is important for the anaesthesiologist in order to judge airway security.	After succeeding in taking the blood pressure comes the opening of the mouth, which again is demonstrated by the doctor (**modelling**).
I complimented him again and then I took a chair and sat next to him, and because he had been so brave and did so well so many times, I sang him a song: *„Süss fel nap, fényes nap, kertek alatt a ludaim megfagynak" (a very well-known song for children about the sunshine).* ... and once again, while I was swinging my waist back and forth, I asked him, *"would you like to sing with me?"*	**Repeated** compliment and then the doctor sits down next to the patient (**pacing**) and starts to sing, which she justifies with the fact that it is the young man's reward for his courage and ability. The simple and familiar song follows again, while the doctor joins the patient's back-and-forth movement (**pacing**), and then she invites him to sing together (**leading**).

Original story	Note
And I touched his left shoulder and sang again, and he was swinging with me, back and forth, back and forth with his waist, and his mother joined in the singing and in the movement too. We moved our heads too. We repeated it for a couple of times and then I put my hand on his shoulder and said: *"That will do, now we stop."*	Hand on the shoulder again, singing and moving together: the mother joins in this hamonious cooperation: the procedure of **passing the rapport** deepens. Repeating the singing and the movement is important: the situation becomes understandable and predictable, giving a **sense of control.** The episode is closed by the doctor's simple, **direct suggestion** (that will do), which can indicate both the closure of that particular situation and the successful cooperation in the future (**future orientation**). It all mediates the fact that she is in control, she knows what she is doing, and the situation is structured by her.
"Next time when we meet in the surgery room, we will sing again like this, and there will be a microphone too, and your mom can also be with us if you want her to."	The doctor, referring to the surgery, forecasts the currently experienced cooperation, again with a determined, **direct suggestion** (**future orientation**). She entrusts the decision about whether the mother should be with them to the young man (**sense of control**). This statement indicates the change of **rapport**: "we will surely cooperate now, the only question is whether you mom should come with us, the decision is yours" – as this tricky offer could be translated. All in all, that is also a **double-bind**: we are definitely going to cooperate, with or without your mom.

Original story	Note
"The morning you will come to the hospital, you have to take your regular medicine with a little water at home. You can change into pyjamas in the surgery department if you want to. But if you don't, you can stay in your ordinary clothes. Your mom will get some green trousers and shirts; this is what I'm going to wear too. At half past eight, the nurse will take you to the door of the surgery room, that's where we will meet."	The doctor tells the information about the surgery (**informing**) facing them, but still talking directly to the young man: after all, she promised that everything would happen just as he wants. The return for the surgery is planted in another **double-bind** (in green clothes or in ordinary ones). The details about the surgery are important (**informing**), especially those related to the time when the young man and his mother will not be with the doctor yet. These things would be relaxing (the clothes are green indeed, it is really the nurse who escorts them, etc).
"We're going in together, your mom will hold your hand all along, we will sing a little, then you will fall asleep. When you wake up, your mom will be holding your hand, we will take you back into the ward, and if you get hungry or thirsty, you can have breakfast, anything you want. Your mom will know what you would like to eat, she will be right next to you all along, because you might fall asleep once again for a little while, and when you've had enough rest, you can get up, walk, you'll go back home by car, just as you've arrived."	A detailed description of everything the young man will experience while he is conscious. The doctor emphasises the circumstances which are important to the patient: the closeness of his mother, the eating, and the car (**pacing**).
"Nothing will hurt, only your face will feel a bit numb. It's all right, isn't it?" We filled in the missing data on the patient's medical form, the mom signed the informed consent form about the anaesthesia, and then they left, holding hands, smiling.	The lack of pain is also promised to the patient and then he is asked for permission (**sense of control**).

Original story	**Note**
We met at the entrance of the surgery room the next morning. The boy was coming hand in hand with his mother, wearing pyjamas and a green surgery hat and smiling. To my surprise, the mother did not want to come into the surgery room, she said that she would stop there, and held out her sons's hand. *"Hi Dénes! Such a nice hat you have!"* I said hi, and meanwhile, he took my hand held out towards him. He did not speak, nor did he look at me. I caressed his shoulders with my other hand, and we left. Dénes was walking beside me, his head bent down, squeezing my hand.	It is an unexpected change that the mother does not want to go into the surgery room, but the doctor is not struck by that, she calls the patient by his name, gives a compliment, then holds out her hand, which the boy takes. Moreover, he follows the doctor to the surgery room (**rapport**). Here comes the real effect of the process of building raport, which was so carefully carried out by the doctor the previous time. Caressing the shoulder reminds the patient of the previous cooperation, calmness, and safety.
We entered the surgery room. The surgeon and the anaestheologist assistant were doing their jobs, they were not paying attention to us, and the surgeon assistant had left. I had already arranged it with them. I explained to my assistant what we were going to do and in which order. Everything was already prepared, so when we entered the room, there was peace and calmness and everything was about consistency and safety.	The colleagues' behaviour is exemplary, the patient does not have to divide his attention, and it is all about his rapport with the doctor.
I told him, "now we sit up here", and I sat up on the surgery table covered with green sheets. I asked him to sit next to me and sing with me just as we did the day before. He was holding my hands all along, but he was not squeezing it anymore. He sat up next to me and squeezed my hand again.	The doctor invites the patient to do the already familiar, well-practiced singing, and she sets an example for the young man with her position (**modelling effect, repetition, pacing**). The patient's hand squeeze must indicate his level of calmness and sense of safety, which is an important sign for the doctor.
"Dénes, you can hold my hand with both of yours if you want to." And he took my hand with both of his hands and I caressed his shoulder with my left hand.	Holding a hand with both hands is the gesture of absolute giving and seeking for safety, just as it was with the mother last time. Caressing the shoulder is for deepening the calmness again.

Original story	Note
I told him once again, calmly and slowly: *"We are going to sing now, and here is the microphone I promised. You are going to fall asleep and we are going to remove that lump from you face. You will wake up and your mom will be holding your hand, we will go back to the ward, and when you're completely awake, you can eat and drink whatever you'd like to."*	The voice tone is also about calmness (**rhythm and pauses**) and everything that is about to happen is repeated again (**repetition, informing**), focused again on the elements most important to the patient (**pacing**).
The assistant gave me the transparent mask. Dénes was sitting on my right side, just like the previous day, I caressed his shoulder, took the mask in my left hand, and started to sing: "*Süss fel nap…*", and started to swing back and forth, dangling my feet back and forth too, and he was swinging with me and trying to sing. The assistant turned up the sleeping gas (sevoran) on the anaesthetic machine and I was holding the mask so that Dénes could sing into it.	The promised "microphone", the caressing of the shoulder, the singing, and the movements are all familiar elements: they are helping to begin the anaesthesia.

Original story	Note
I started to feel soon that the squeeze of his hands is weakening and he starts drooping, so I could hold the mask right to his face. The assistant held the patient from behind and we called the surgeon's mate who helped us to lay him down. Then the vein security with vygon (on top of which there is a vent for medication) was put in the right lower arm, careful that it does not get into crook of the arm. Pulzoxymetria, EKG, noninvasive monitoring of blood pressure, sleeping gas, ventilation, and during kapnographia iv. Multiple intervention was needed: body mass proportioned propofol, 1 mg midazolam, and after giving 1 ml fentanyl, I placed a laryngeal mask on his face. During assisted ventilation by sevoral inhalatio ballon, I asked the surgeon to inject local anaesthesia. The surgery took 20 minutes, at the end, I removed the laryngeal mask by sufficient spontaneous ventilation in deep narcosis and he then got 100% oxygen through the mask for a few minutes. After that, we placed him on a bed and pushed him out to the hall where the mom was already waiting for him.	The anaesthesia is successful.
The mom was talking to him and holding his hands. Dénes opened his eyes for a few seconds first, then fell asleep again for a couple of minutes, smiling. During this time, we carried him back to the ward and put him onto his bed. By that time, he turned to his side, his eyes were searching for his mother, and he held out his hands for her. She sat down next to him and caressed his head. After about half an hour, he woke up and asked for his cocoa drink. He was feeling good, touched his face with his head, and felt the bandage but didn't pick at it.	The young man and his mom can reunite.

Original story	Note
I complimented him again for being so brave and for singing so beautifully, and because of that, I gave him a blown-up rubber glove with five fingers, with a mouth, teeth, eyes, and eyebrows painted on it with permanent marker. It was also because the parent did not bring any toys, but so that Dénes could play with this "balloon".	Compliment again, a gift, and gradually returning the **rapport** to the mother.
The young man was allowed to go home in four hours' time, around midday. He could also keep the disposable green hat. The parents signed the report. I said goodbye to Dénes, who didn't say anything, but he waved at me, smiling.	The operation turned out to be a positive experience instead of "holding him down".

Initial situation	Goal
– Negative trance occupied by fear – Unsuccessful attempt at administering local anaesthesia	– Building cooperation – Dealing with the mother's rapport – Preparing the circumstances for anaesthesia

DESCRIBER OF THE CASE: Vass Zsuzsa Dr., Neurologist, Anesthesiologist, Intensive-Therapy Specialist.

THE FIRST EDITION: Exam paper for the postgraduate training program on Suggestive Communication in Somatic Medicine, co-organised by the Hungarian Association of Hypnosis and Semmelweis University School of Medicine, Budapest.

Describers of the Cases

Benedek, Zsolt; Anaesthesiological Assistant
Biró, Eszter; Counselling Psychologist
Bloch-Szentágothai, Katalin Dr.; Anesthesiologist, Hypnotherapist
Diószeghy, Csaba, Dr.; Anaesthesiologist-Intensive Therapy, Oxycologist-Emergency Specialist
Gyurkovics, Zoltánné; Midwife
K. Szilágyi, Adrienn; Clinical Psychologist
Kertész, Krisztina; Dietician
Kondor, Katalin; Midwife, Perinatal Advisor
Kónyi, Olga Dr.; Neonatologist
Kovács, Gabriella Dr.; Anesthesiologist, Intensive Care Specialist
Kovács, Zoltán Ambrus Dr.; Psychiatrist
Magassy, Réka; Midwife Student
McKenna, Mhairi; Dr., Hypnotherapist
Pazonyiné, Balázs Zsuzsa; Mental Hygienist
Rákócziné, Krämer Ágnes; Midwife, Perinatal Advisor, Lactation Specialist (IBCLC)
Radányi, Éva Dr.; Dentist and Periodontist
Székely, Gábor Dr.; Anesthesiologist, Intensive-Therapy Specialist, Psychologist
Tóth, Katalin Judit Dr.; Anesthesiologist, Intensive Care Specialist, Pediatrician and Pediatric Neurologist
Varga, Katalin Dr.; Psychologist
Varga, Krisztina Dr.; Dentist
Vass, Gabriella; Midwife
Vass, Zsuzsa Dr.; Neurologist, Anesthesiologist, Intensive-Therapy Specialist

*

Acknowledgement

My sincere thanks to those who helped to prepare and improve this manuscript:

Nikolett Béleczki, Zack Boukydis, Gabrielle Cooper, Julianna Hedberg, Lilla Hegedűs, Judit Osvát, Imre Szabolics, and Márta Zakó.

Consciousness and Human Systems

Edited by Dagmar Eigner, Günther Fleck, Shulamith Kreitler and László Ropoly

Vol. 1 Shulamith Kreitler / Günther Fleck / László Ropoly / Dagmar Eigner (eds.): Systems of Logic and the Construction of Order. 2012.

Vol. 2 Dagmar Eigner (ed.): Consciousness: Cultural and Therapeutic Perspectives. 2012.

Vol. 3 Katalin Varga: Communication Strategies in Medical Settings. Challenging Situations and Practical Solutions. 2015.

www.peterlang.com

www.ingramcontent.com/pod-product-compliance
Ingram Content Group UK Ltd.
Pitfield, Milton Keynes, MK11 3LW, UK
UKHW020121290926
15471UKWH00003B/202

9 783631 662458